BiTCH

BiTCH

BiTCH

Copyright © 2006 Omnibus Press
(A Division of Music Sales Limited)

Cover and book designed by
Chloë Alexander
Picture research by Sarah Bacon
and Matt Guido

ISBN 13: 978.1.84609.635.8
1.84609.635.9
Order No: OP51590

Exclusive Distributors
Music Sales Limited,
14/15 Berners Street,
London, W1T 3LJ.

Music Sales Corporation,
257 Park Avenue SouthCopyright © 2006

Macmillan Distribution Services,
53 Park West Drive,
Derrimut, Vic 3030,
Australia.

Printed by: MPG Books Ltd, Bodmin, Cornwall

A catalogue record for this book is available
from the British Library.

Visit Omnibus Press on the web at
www.omnibuspress.com

All photographs courtesy of London Features
International with the exception of the
following:

Page 69 Ian Dury photo by Victor Watts/Rex
Features
Page 125 Phil Lewis photo by Paul
Natkin/WireImage
Page 129 Matt Cameron photo by Karen Mason
Blair/Corbis
Page 145 Walter Trout photo by James
Dittiger/Redferns
Page 155 Billy Childish photo by John Dee/Rex
Features
Page 165 Andy Nicholson photo by Tabatha
Fireman/Redferns
Page 167 Jamie Cook, Arctic Monkeys photo
by Pat Pope/Retna Pictures

Every effort has been made to trace the
copyright holders of the photographs in this
book but one or two were unreachable. We
would be grateful if the photographers
concerned would contact us.

BiTCH

NSULTS, ABUSE AND OUTRAGE – ALL IN THE NAME OF FAME!

BiTCH

COMPILED BY SUSAN BLACK

BiTCH

OMNIBUS PRESS

London/New York/Paris/Sydney/Copenhagen/Madrid/Tokyo

INTRODUCTION

"I think it's sort of funny how you have to be doing coke off the ass of a stripper to be perceived as not boring these days," Gwyneth Paltrow told a *Guardian* interviewer early in 2006.

The Hollywood actress was reacting to allegations that Coldplay, the enormously successful band led by her husband Chris Martin, might lack cutting edge credentials, the kind of thing that Creation boss Allan McGee was referring to when he suggested that the band produced "music for bedwetters".

Bitchiness has been part and parcel of the pop world since Frank Sinatra saw Elvis Presley hip-swivelling his way into the hearts of teenagers in the 1950s, and was famously scathing about rock'n'roll, the new music that would see his own style take a permanent back seat. "It is the most brutal, ugly, desperate, vicious form of expression it has been my misfortune to hear," he said.

It didn't go away, though, and neither did the bitchiness, or sour grapes, which this book celebrates. In the Sixties and Seventies rock musicians were generally kind to one another, this being the peace and love generation, but the punk explosion changed all that, it being more or less mandatory for the new generation with spiky hair and torn t-shirts to slag off the older generation of old farts. Maybe it hit a peak as an art form in the eighties, when the likes of Boy George turned his camp tongue on all and sundry and the pop scene reflected the time-honoured tradition started in Thirties Hollywood by Bette Davis. There was something distinctly theatrical in his witty, if not catty, denounce-ment of enemies and icons alike, George displaying a turn of phrase to die for and often stimulating similarly acid comments from his targets.

The nineties was somewhat less vintage for connoisseurs of bitchiness, although the Brit-pop wars brought the likes of Noel Gallagher (Oasis), Damon Albarn (Blur) and Jarvis Cocker (Pulp) to the coalface. In terms of 'noughties bitches', we have surely unearthed a gem in the comely shape of Charlotte 'Voice of an Angel' Church, who appears to have a quote for every occasion... if not yet the hits to back them up. Sir Elton John, with more hits than he can handle, has also proved his staying power as an enduringly lovable bitch of our times.

The world of heavy metal has reverberated to a number of broadsides as guitar heroes rubbish their rivals. The likes of Motörhead's Lemmy have raised the bar to a considerable extent, though Ozzy Osbourne and his family have been more than content to limbo under it when the occasion has demanded. Children Kelly and Jack and wife Sharon have also contributed their share of reality TV humour.

On the other hand, the advent of the TV-created *Pop Idol* has led to a rash of white-bread stars unwilling or unable to bite the hand that feeds them. It's been left to the judges, the omnipotent Simon Cowell – the most powerful man in showbusiness today? – and previously mentioned uber-bitch Sharon Osbourne to lead the way, even if their remarks have often been aimed at defenceless/talentless newcomers rather than those more worthy of their barbs.

As the new millennium continues merrily on, favoured objects of pop-star scorn have included former Libertines singer Pete Doherty, now of Babyshambles, who seems to have made a career of living out the second part of his new band's name, and the Rolling Stones for having the temerity to rock on past bus-pass age. The odds on which will give out first have only been equalled by the numbers of celebs willing to venture an opinion.

Like most of us, pop stars have always revelled in others' misfortunes – the raison d'etre of the tabloid press – and have often not been slow to express the same. That situation is unlikely to change and, with the internet and rolling news channels giving them a yet broader canvas for their bitchiness, the stream of invective – witty, worthy or otherwise – is unlikely to slow down any time yet.

Indeed, if one conclusion can be drawn from our motley collection of moans, groans and verbal missiles it is surely this – no matter how privileged, pampered or pecunious a pop star, they will always find something (or someone] to complain about.

Long may they bitch!

Susan Black

THE SIXTIES – PEACE AND LOVE

We don't like their sound.
Groups of guitars are on the
way out.
Dick Rowe, Decca A&R manager,
turning down the Beatles, 1962

The Beatles are
not merely
awful... they are
so unbelievably
horrible, so
appallingly
unmusical, so
dogmatically insensitive
to the magic of art that they
qualify as crowned heads of
antimusic.
William F Buckley, writer, 1964

We've played many palaces,
including Frisco's Cow
Palace. But never this one
before. It's a keen pad and I
like the staff. I thought
they'd be dukes and things

but they were just fellas.
Paul McCartney on Buckingham
Palace, 1965

I don't know which will go
first – rock'n'roll or
Christianity.
◄ John Lennon, 1966

The amusing
thing about this
is its supreme
unimportance – after
it's all over, and they've
outsold everyone else in
history, The Monkees will still
leave absolutely no mark on
American music.
Crawdaddy! magazine, 1967

I've been imitated so well
I've heard people copy
my mistakes.
Jimi Hendrix, 1968

*The rest of the group is fine
but the singer will have to go.*
Eric Easton, taking over as Rolling Stones manager, 1962

The audiences were hostile to what we did. They gave us a bad time. Now, historically, musicians have felt real hurt if the audience expressed displeasure with their performance. They apologised and tried to make people love them. We didn't do that. We told the audience to get fucked.
Frank Zappa, 1968 ◤

I was washing dishes at the Greyhound bus station at the time. I couldn't talk back to my boss man. He would bring all these pots back for me to wash, and one day I said, 'I've got to do something to stop this man bringing back all these pots to me to wash,' and I said, 'Awap bop a lup bop a wop bam boom, take 'em out!'
Little Richard, 1969

....

They're about to poke their genitals into our cream cheese moon right now. That's my eye; the moon is part of me. Why don't they poke it in the sun? They're not very daring.'
Captain Beefheart, 1969

....

I think music is the main interest of the younger people. It doesn't really matter about the older people now because they're finished anyway.
George Harrison, 1968

When I was in school, geezers that were snappy dressers and got chicks would always like to talk about my nose. This seemed to be the biggest thing in my life: my fucking nose, man.

Pete Townshend, 1968

The most loving parents and relatives commit murder with smiles on their faces. They force us to destroy the person we really are: a subtle kind of murder.

Jim Morrison, 1970

I opened the door for a lot of people, and they just ran through and left me holding the knob.

Bo Diddley, 1970

He stole my music but he gave me my name.

Muddy Waters on Mick Jagger, 1970

When they get you in the record business, someone gonna rip you anyway so that don't bother me. If you don't rip me, she gonna rip me, and if she don't rip me, she gonna rip me, so I'm gonna get ripped, so you don't be bothered by that, because people round you gonna rip you if they can.

Muddy Waters, 1970

I'm not a rock star. I'm a soft person. I'm not a rock.'

◄ Captain Beefheart, 1971

For a nation that can put a man on the moon, it isn't much of a problem to find a cure for heroin addiction – not if they really want to.

Keith Richards, 1972

There are only forty people in the world and five of them are hamburgers.

Captain Beefheart, 1975

I get bored, you see. There was this time in Saskatoon, Canada. It was another 'Oliday Inn, and I was bored. Now, when I get bored, I rebel. I said, 'FUCK IT, FUCK THE LOT OF YA!' And I took out me 'atchet and chopped the 'otel room to bits. The television. The chairs. The dresser. The cupboard doors. The bed. The lot of it. Ah-ha-ha-HAHAHAHAHAHAHAH! It happens all the time.

Keith Moon, 1973 ◣

I couldn't bear to end up as an Elvis Presley and sing in Las Vegas with all those housewives and old ladies come in with their handbags. It's really sick.

Mick Jagger, 1972

I still like black music, disco music... 'Shame, Shame, Shame' or 'Rock Your Baby'

—I'd give my eye-tooth to have written that. But I never could. I am too literal to write 'Rock Your Baby'. I wish I could. I'm too intellectual, even though I'm not really an intellectual.

John Lennon, 1975

I wasn't at all surprised Ziggy Stardust made my career. I packaged a totally credible plastic rock star – much better than any sort of Monkees fabrication. My plastic rocker was much more plastic than anybody's.

David Bowie, 1976

Nobody's too old to Rock'n'Roll but there is a difference between being 40 and being 30.

Ian Anderson, Jethro Tull, 1976

You're always frustrated, you don't have the chance to do a song on the album, like

A piece of cardboard that they drag round on a trolley.

Johnny Rotten, on the Queen, 1977

The Beatles did with Ringo and George, or like Led Zeppelin, where everybody was given a chance to contribute. There never is a chance with the Stones.

Bill Wyman, 1975

....

Los Angeles is awful – like Liverpool with palm trees.

Johnny Rotten, 1977

....

A toss-pot is even lower than a jerk-off. A queer is a pansy. If you don't know that, it's just an indication of how fucking stupid you Americans are.

Johnny Rotten, 1977

....

Being in Fleetwood Mac is more like being in group therapy.

Mick Fleetwood, 1977

....

I'm not pleased at Johnny Rotten, who says all nasty things about me. I know that he feels he has to because I'm, along with the Queen, you know, one of the best things England's got. Me and the Queen.

Mick Jagger, 1977

....

They're quite a commune, Virgin Records. A load of groupies as secretaries... all Hampstead hippies.

Johnny Rotten, 1978

....

I've worked me bloody way into the record business, and now I've got teachers again, slapping wrists every time I don't quite pull it off.

Paul McCartney, 1978

....

Charlie Watts never could play a solo. And don't believe

Music is like being a bank clerk.

Kate Bush, 1978

him when he says he only joined the band on a temporary basis, ha-ha. It was the only gig he could get.

Mick Jagger, 1978

....

My teeth – I don't like how they stand out. I always think of arranging them but I don't have time. Besides, I'm perfect.

Freddie Mercury, Queen, 1980

....

You can't trust politicians. It doesn't matter to me who makes a political speech. It's all lies... and it applies to any rock star who wants to make a political speech as well.

Bob Geldof, 1978

....

People ask us, are you punk or what? That's bullshit. I don't care what colour your hair is, what clothes you wear. If you dig the music, that's what it's all about.

Lemmy, Motörhead, 1978

....

Is he just doing a bad Elvis pout, or was he born that way?

Freddie Mercury on Billy Idol, 1979

....

I am very nice to people. I mean, I have my bad side, but I don't think I'm really nasty. I think there are a lot of people who think that maybe I am really. Fuck them.

Debbie Harry, Blondie, 1980

....

I don't like people like Rod Stewart and Elton John, and I don't like the way they carry on. I get very upset at being identified with that kind of person.

Mick Jagger, 1978

....

Having been there in the Seventies in LA isn't it amazing that the only ones that mattered are all dead – everyone else is in an imitatative state of a dying animal.

Darby Crash, the Germs, 1980

....

In Glasgow, a kid climbed up the toilet pipe, stuck his hand into the dressing room window and shouted 'Touch me! Touch me!' so I answered him, 'Go fuck yourself, I'm not the Pope!'
Ian Dury, 1980 ◥

Spandau Ballet... Amateur hour!! Stuff like jamming at rehearsals which you'd chuck out and wouldn't consider putting on plastic. To them, that's a *tour de force*.
Johnny Rotten, 1981

I think the New Romantic thing is pathetic, they see clothes as the be-all and end-all. I'm not a wedding cake. I've suffered for what I am, and feel bitter.
Pete Burns, Dead or Alive, 1981

I have no faith in politics, and place no value in leadership of any kind.
Sting, 1981

I never really liked The Sex Pistols because they were a heavy metal band.
Edwyn Collins, Orange Juice, 1982

I don't get on with them at all, especially the ones I meet in this business. They're usually just cheap whores looking for a lay. I dislike them intensely.
Toyah Wilcox on women, 1981

Current pop music is depressingly safe and shallow and completely disposable, People are so insecure that they're playing music that's boring – music that has no sex or aggression or emotion. Present pop is all calculated.

Siouxsie, Siouxsie & The Banshees, 1982

···

I get called out for having a bodyguard, but sometimes it's necessary. I nearly had my chest ripped off once... imagine losing a tit to a total stranger?

Debbie Harry, Blondie, 1982

···

I'm not hip and I'm glad, because I hate hip. Hip doesn't last. I was never hip.

Meat Loaf, 1982

···

The woman from *The Sun* said 'Oh Annabella., everyone in the office wants to know – are you a virgin or not?' I said 'It's none of your bloody business!'

Annabella Lu Win, Bow Wow Wow, 1982

···

Rock music is at the stage where it has become part of the establishment... How can you be a rebel, when rebellion is the norm? Therefore rock'n'roll has lost its power as a revolutionary force. I think bands who call themselves revolutionary are playing at it. They're having no effect whatsoever.

Sting, 1982

···

It's very much like being a robot, being in a group.

Joe Strummer, The Clash, 1982

Sometimes a woman can really persuade you to make an asshole of yourself.

Rod Stewart, 1982

> A more fickle, paranoid, self-congratulatory bunch of failed musicians you'd be hard put to find anywhere.
> The Chords on the music press, 1982

All this [studio] equipment is the great equaliser, doing away with all that virtuoso crap.
Martin Rushent,
Human League
producer, 1982

I might have to trick myself [into writing a hit single] by pretending to write a song for Billy Joel or Foreigner and then kind of sneak up on it and record it for myself.
Randy Newman, 1982

When we were in Calcutta, I realised how irrelevant, what an empty bubble of space the whole fashion thing is.
Stewart Copeland, The Police, 1982

Springsteen writes about cars; I write about my chick. Who the fuck cares about what gas pedal you've got in your car?
Willie de Ville, Mink de Ville, 1982

> People go on about how awful radio is in America, but it's not the radio's fault – it's the witless bozos who make the records.
> ◀ Nick Lowe, 1982

All the band bring incense when we're in the studio because they can't stand the smell of my feet.
Captain Sensible, The Damned, 1982

> I thought [President] Reagan would have been more sympathetic to the arts, seeing as he started out feeding monkeys in movies.
> Chris Stein, Blondie, 1982

There are problems with fame: like buying underwear at Woolworth's and disappointing the girl behind the counter because you didn't get extra large.

Stewart Copeland, The Police, 1982

....

I don't bite the head off chickens or frighten horses, but I've survived in this business for years. I like gardening and growing vegetables at home.

Tony Banks, Genesis, 1982

....

There are too many microwave bands around. They look pretty good on the surface, but as soon as you stick your knife and fork in...

Martin Fry, ABC, 1982

....

It's my job, I get paid for making records, writing songs. It's not much different from other jobs, I mean a recording studio is not much different from a factory. It's just a factory for music.

Van Morrison, 1982

....

In the States, if you put out something that sounds like it was recorded in a toilet, which is what rock'n'roll is essentially, you can't get it on the radio. The Top 100 is the same old schlock they've been peddling for ten years.

John Hiatt, 1982

....

I went down to see The Police and was very impressed by them. Somebody took us into the

I'd always hated the idea of touring; crisp packets lying around the dressing room and people trying to sell you drugs.

Mark Fox, Haircut 100, 1982

dressing room to meet them and it was very nice. But from then on, all I've read in the papers were snidey little remarks about us.

Mick Jones, Foreigner, 1982

....

I think there's nothing worse than appearing on *Top Of The Pops* if you're over thirty-five. I find that shocking, really sad. It's not dignified.

Sting, The Police, 1982 ▶

....

I bought a synthesiser to see how they work. I got some bird noises and sea sounds, but they're shit, synthesisers. No-one needs them.

Captain Sensible, 1982

....

This time America's been really different because all the romanticism's gone. First two times, I came with a head full of Kerouac and

Tom Waits and Woody Guthrie – but that's all out of the window now. Now I see America as ugly, plasticated, horrific…

Joe Strummer, The Clash, 1982

....

When we were on tour supporting Shakin' Stevens, his manager gave us a list of stuff we couldn't wear – like pink jackets, black trousers, or denims. We actually spoke to him once, for about five minutes out of twenty-eight days.

Bobby Cotton, The Jets, 1982

I will sit down with anybody that has criticised my work negatively; I will sit down with them and make them eat shit. Figuratively speaking, of course!

August Darnell, Kid Creole and The Coconuts, 1982

....

If you want to sing about innocence or truth, or even God, nobody wants to know.

Bono, U2, 1983

Basically, the rest of The Specials were a load of prats.

Terry Hall, Fun Boy Three (and ex-Specials), 1982

....

Every fucking art student that plays out of tune gets a record deal.

Willy de Ville, Mink de Ville, 1982

....

Queen's audience hated us. I couldn't imagine anyone feeling so vitriolic towards a band. Some of the people down in the front were vibrating with the pain of wanting to kill us and not being able to get near enough to do it.

Julian Cope, The Teardrop Explodes, 1982 ◣

....

America's the land of the fat arse. The birds are pretty rough, but they give good head.

Matthew Ashman, Bow Wow Wow, 1982

....

I had bailiffs round my house last year to pick up the television and the furniture. I was standing there with my cricket bat and wouldn't let them in. I'd have killed them. I said they'd only get that stuff over my dead body.

Captain Sensible, the Damned, 1982

....

Punk changed the [music) business, but only temporarily. English pop music is still about trivia and homosexuals, isn't it?!!

Johnny Rotten, 1983

You know what the Italians are like...
fucking chaos!
Johnny Rotten, 1983

I can spot empty flattery and know exactly where I stand. In the end it's really only my own approval or disapproval that means anything.

Agnetha Faltskog, ex-Abba, 1983

If I had a time machine, I'd go back and beat up Julius Caesar and I'd have a right go at Henry VIII. He was a male chauvinist wanker... I'd kick him right in the nuts. And I'd go back and circumcise Hitler – just to wind him up!
Captain Sensible, The Damned, 1982 ◥

There's one thing I'd like to do now and that's go back to my old dole office, open a bottle of champagne and spray it in their faces.
Biff Byford, Saxon, 1982

The Police is a pop band, definitely not a rock band.

We write music that window cleaners can whistle.
Sting. 1983

I got a message from Boy George through Peter Powell, saying let's be friends. I said 'fuck off, I don't speak to men in dresses'.
Pete Burns, Dead or Alive, 1984

The world dictates that heteros make love, while gays have sex.
Boy George, 1984

You are what you eat, and who wants to be a lettuce?
Pete Burns, on vegetarians, 1984

Lionel Richie... he's got a chin like an ironing board.
Pete Burns, Dead or Alive, 1984

OK, there's always the odd letter or comment like, 'If you don't play ten 'Metal Militia's on every album then it's not Metallica and it's not good'. But we're doing what we're doing the way we feel at a certain time. The band had matured and we're still learning. If people think we're wimping out then fuck 'em, we don't need that kinda shit.
Lars Ulrich, Metallica, 1984

The mid-Seventies were probably the hardest times for us. Drugs never really interested me at all, but at point in the Seventies period, it was 'cool man' and all the audience would sit on the floor, stoned. There were all these progressive bands doing 10- or 15-minute solos with their enormous gear.

We were more bizarre than they were, with our bright loud jackets, singing away with our little amps, doing three-minute numbers!
▼ Shakin' Stevens, 1984

The charts are a very boring experience. That's the

The thing about [Boy] George is, he's always been a big-headed, arrogant bastard – so success hasn't really changed him!
Jon Moss, Culture Club, 1985

annoying thing about being in the charts at the moment – it sort of doesn't count, because they're all so awful.

Neil Tennant, Pet Shop Boys, 1985

There are indeed worse groups than Modern Romance, but can anybody seriously think of one?

Morrissey, 1985

People say I've set back the women's movement 30 years – but I think that women weren't ashamed of their bodies in the fifties. They luxuriated in their femininity and believed whole-heartedly in it. Women aren't like men. They can do things that men can't, mentally and physically. If people don't get the humour in my act, then they don't want to get it.

Madonna, 1985

A drunken goat could direct a Duran Duran video.

Morrissey, 1985

There was an incredible amount of wealth in the studio. People were singing, 'Feed the World', and saying it was the most worthwhile thing they'd ever done. And I thought, 'Did you actually do anything else about it?' I'll bet most of the people there didn't even go and buy the record.

▼George Michael, on Band Aid, 1985

Basically, I hate pop stars unless they're me or personal friends of mine.

Shane MacGowan, the Pogues, 1985

Boy George reminds me of an aubergine –
all shiny and plump!

Paul Young, 1985

I never wanted Band Aid to go on for a long time. Then it would become an institution like ICI or the NME.
Bob Geldof, 1985

Band Aid is undiscussable.
Morrissey, January 1985

My pet hate is The Smiths... they're so pathetic! What are they on about? I don't know!
Ozzy Osbourne, 1985

Honestly, all this clean image stuff really gets on my nerves. Like people in America were coming up to me and saying, 'George, I'm really pleased you're giving our kids some clean, harmless fun,' and I'd be going 'AAAARGH! No!! I don't want this'.
George Michael, Wham!, 1985

I saw *Paris, Texas* and I thought it was rubbish, actually. It was like looking at a lot of postcards. Ry Cooder is a very fine guitarist, but the impression I got was that it [the soundtrack] took him ten minutes.
Mark Knopfler, Dire Straits, 1985

I really think autographs are daft. What do they want them for? What's the point? But you can't ask them that – they'd just think you were being snotty.
Bernard Sumner, New Order, 1985

The telly here is appalling. It's disgraceful, no imagination at all. *EastEnders* **is the worse thing I've seen in my life.**
Johnny Rotten, 1986

There are only two bands in the whole world that are any good – us and Motörhead.
Dee Dee Ramone, The Ramones, 1985

*People don't like me because I'm so smart-assed.
I probably wouldn't like myself if I didn't
know myself better!*

Bob Geldof, Boomtown Rats, 1985

The Who and the Stones are revolting. All they're good for is making money.
Johnny Rotten, 1986

I can't actually play any musical instrument properly. I can't read music. And here's the *New York Times* calling me the new George Gershwin...
Elvis Costello, 1986 ▶

I've had a lot of dead weight around me over the years. Now I come to think of it, most of the people I've worked with have done nothing since. I've destroyed their lives!
Johnny Rotten, 1986

If anyone saw me nude, I think they'd be sick. I just don't have the sort of body that should be seen without clothes.
Patsy Kensit, 1986

I'm bored stiff with people complaining about the French and never going there, or just going to the obvious places. They have no concept of what the French are at all. I do... and they're awful!
Johnny Rotten, 1986

Big tits on page three are really damaging to our society.
Siobhan Fahey, Bananarama, 1986

27

Comparing Marilyn Monroe with Madonna is like comparing Raquel Welch to the back of a bus.

Boy George, 1986

Boy George makes me sick!

Madonna, 1986

He [Jimmy Somerville] thinks I should do more for the gay community, and he's right... I should strangle him! That's the best thing anyone could do for them!

Marc Almond, 1986

It was good keeping Wham! off the top for a week. After all their boasting about how they were going to go straight in at Number One, and sticking their necks out like that. There's nothing more unattractive in an artist than a false sense of importance.

Simon Le Bon, Duran Duran 1986 ◥

Toyah? Stick to acting.

Paul Weller, 1986

Samantha Fox? Bleugggh!'

Paul Weller, 1986

Kim Wilde – who?

Paul Weller, 1986

It's never been an ambition of mine to be a mega pop star. All I ever really wanted was to headline at [London club] Dingwalls – and I never even got to do that!

Alison Moyet, 1986

I think it's kinda depressing that Kirk [Hammett] got a free ride to number one in your magazine's [Metal Forces] readers' poll in '84 because of my guitar solos from the 'No Life Till Leather' demo.

Dave Mustaine, ex-Metallica guitarist, 1986

One of my regrets is not being discovered earlier. I was a 15 year old working in a South Wales glove factory when rock'n'roll came out in 1955... but I had to wait until I was 24, and by then it was too late.

Tom Jones, 1986

I'm sick of the right, I'm sick of the left, sick of Lenin, Marx, Reaganomics, Friedman and Keynes. Most of all, I'm sick of the middle. We need new dreams tonight. But where are the new dreamers?

Bono, U2, 1986

The music business is like having your head put in a dog turd.

Shane MacGowan, the Pogues, 1986

I wake up some nights and I think, 'Orchestral Manoeuvres In The Dark'!? What a stupid name! Why did we pick that one?

Andy McCluskey, Orchestral Manoeuvres In The Dark, 1986

We used to have all these girls taking pictures of themselves and sending them in. We had this thing called the Ugly Board like Reader's Wives, only worse.

Mark O'Toole, Frankie Goes To Hollywood, 1986

I won't speak to the teen mags because all they want to talk about is hairspray and stuff, and it's all just a crock of shit. I don't want to sell the band on that.

Jon Bon Jovi, Bon Jovi, 1986

My bullshit is worth more than others' diamonds.

Lou Reed, 1986

We hate studio photo sessions.
It's an insult to creative taste. We don't understand
why people want these sorts of pictures anyway.

Aha, 1986

Mothers still hide their kids from me in airports.
Alice Cooper, 1986

You go to a supermarket and you see a faggot behind the fucking cash register, you don't want him to handle your potatoes. It's true. It's paranoid, but that's the way it is. There's a lotta religious people, of course, who feel that this is God's work. God's saying 'No more butt fucking or we're gonna getcha!'
Neil Young on AIDS, 1986 ◣

In the late Sixties, a certain group of people got so far up their own asses, they shit all over themselves.
Ian Astbury, the Cult, 1986

What's Billy Bragg gonna change? He ain't doing nothing. All he's doing is telling people that Thatcher's a cow. Well, I think most people know that, don't they?
Rat Scabies, The Damned, 1986

The Fun Boy Three were just totally geared to money making. It was a pop group – that's why we had silly haircuts.
Terry Hall, The Colour Field, 1986

If you're in this business for more than five years, you become a boring old fart. These days, I actually don't care one bit of someone likes what we do – I don't care that much about pleasing people.
Brian Travers, UB40, 1986

We got attacked by a religious maniac on this plane from Denver – a fucking loony in cowboy boots and sunglasses that only had one

31

lens. He kept screaming at us, and then a Bible came sailing over and hit the Captain on his head. Then he came over to me and started kicking my ankles and shouting 'Hey, what about the Lord?' I said 'Listen, fuck-face, you kick me again and you're dead!'

Rat Scabies, The Damned, 1986

The biggest misconception people have about me is that I'm stupid.

Billy Idol, 1986

You now have a nation of kids who don't read. The bulk of information that enters their brains comes from television or records... so control over those sources of information is rather attractive to an authoritarian mentality.

Frank Zappa, 1986

People would like to see us crushed and killed. The British love you on the way up, but take greater pleasure in knocking you down once you've arrived at the top.

Mikey Craig, Culture Club, 1986

Because it's such a desperate, dirty sort of place, we resisted the temptation to start singing about politics and how bad it was to be in Birmingham. We were a sort of escapism.

Roger Taylor, Duran Duran, 1986

I am a ham. I've no business in rock'n'roll. I've said over and over again that I'm a classical composer, dishevelling my musical personality by dabbling in rock'n'roll. I'm more interested in symphonic music.

◤ John Cale, 1986

Politicians will fuck you up whoever they are.
They never keep their promises.

Lemmy, Motörhead, 1986

I'm sure if there's a new fascism, it won't come from skinheads and punks. It will come from people who eat granola and believe they know how the world should be.
Eno, 1986

Duff music is killing music, it's as easy as that. Home taping encourages music, so does bootlegging. Enthusiasm encourages.

▲ Jim Kerr, Simple Minds, 1986

What do bands like Tears For Fears and Spandau Ballet feel when they see programmes on Orgreave or Nicaragua or South Africa? I don't see how anybody can see things like that and not be affected in some way.
David Steele, Fine Young Cannibals, 1986

I hate modern design houses – I couldn't live in a Barratt home no matter what incentive they gave me!
Feargal Sharkey, ex-Undertones, 1986

Anybody who takes a twenty minute guitar solo should be shot, and I mean that. If it takes you twenty minutes to say something then don't bother.
Robert Cray, 1986

It's like these artists who say home taping is killing music.

Music paper interviews? I hate to tell ya, but two days after they're printed they're lining the trashcan.

Tom Waits, 1986

All the stuff around now is a load of old pap. It's all suited to Terry Wogan and *Top Of The Pops* and Thatcher and all those things that go hand in hand.

Mick Jones, Big Audio Dynamite, 1986

....

I think the whole concept of interpreting dreams is the biggest wank really. My dreams are very straight forward – very much like my life.

Robert Smith, The Cure, 1986 ▶

....

I think that the old rock'n'roll lifestyle of drink and drugs should die. I'm amazed that rock stars still insist on swallowing bottles

of bourbon and marrying models with big tits but nothing between the ears.

Tony James, Sigue Sigue Sputnik, 1986

....

At the moment in Britain, you've got to be either this week's new band or a revered antique like Phil Collins. Bands which have been around for a few years seem to be falling down a hole in the middle.

Andy McCluskey, Orchestral Manoeuvres In The Dark, 1986

....

Racists make me so sick. I just want to shit on their faces.

Flea, Red Hot Chilli Peppers, 1986

....

The Fine Young Cannibals sound like the contents of Elvis Preseley's draining board.
Tony James, Sigue Sigue Sputnik, 1986

I think The Sex Pistols were the worst thing that's ever happened.
Cliff Richard, 1987

I used to be compared with [Culture Club's] Helen Terry, but that was simply because we were a couple of fat birds.
Alison Moyet, 1987 ▶

Marilyn Monroe was a victim and I'm not. That's why there's really no comparison.
Madonna, 1987

I'm irritated that the world that we live in, and its culture and society, can build and maintain Madonna.
Natalie Merchant, 10,000 Maniacs, 1987

I'm the closest I've been to Paul [McCartney] for the last ten or twelve years. I still love him and I'm going to continue my friendship regardless of his attitude, because I don't have time to screw around.
George Harrison, 1987

Billy Idol has made two or three good records but when he opens his mouth he's still a prat.
Tony James, Sigue Sigue Sputnik, 1986

In America, our record company is run by a pile of complete egocentrics, and they'd say to us, 'Listen, you don't know anything about America, you don't know how America works, trust us.' So I trusted them and ended up looking like a complete slut.

Carol Decker, T'Pau, 1987

If Morrissey's a genius then what's he doing in a fucking pop group?

Shane MacGowan, the Pogues, 1987

When people recognize me they're generally very pleased. If they're not, they call you a wanker or something like that. But I can deal with that, I'm from Newcastle.

Sting, 1987

I never swore as a kid, but when I came into the industry it seemed that every other word heard was the one that began with 'F' and I picked it up, I'm afraid to say.

Cliff Richard, 1987

I've got people who want to kill me and people who want to make love to me, just so they can sell their stories to the newspapers.

Bono, U2, 1987

If we were devastatingly handsome and actually liked one another, we'd probably be the biggest band on earth. As it is, I'm actually quite a decent chap and the rest of the group are complete wankers.

Jools Holland, Squeeze, 1987

The majority of pop stars are complete idiots in every aspect.

Sade, 1987

I've met Bono many times and he's told me several jokes, none of which have been very funny.

Mike Peters, The Alarm, 1987

Each time I come back to England, it hits me how revolting and ridiculous it is. England really is a shithole... and that hurts.
Ali Campbell, UB40, 1987

I looked at the Top Ten and thought, 'I don't want to be in there with those people anyway'. I've never seen such a dreadful mire of crap in all my life!
Mick Hucknall, Simply Red, 1987

There are only two bands in the whole world that are any good – us and Motörhead.
Dee Dee Ramone, The Ramones, 1985

I'm used to being called a raving madman, but it's different for Patricia [Morrison]. It's all very well being the idiot, but being the idiot's lieutenant is no fun at all.
Andrew Eldritch, Sisters of Mercy, 1987

We chose Steve Lillywhite to produce our album because he wasn't as fat and sweaty as our previous producer [Elvis Costello].
◀ Shane MacGowan, The Pogues, 1987

I don't mind that we've moved into the yuppie market. Being a yuppie is

better than being
one of those
people who
wear baseball
caps and try
and pretend
they live on the
street.

Mick Hucknall, Simply Red, 1987 ▶

One company, I
can't remember
which one, put
in a bid for us
without even
hearing the
tape. Then, after
they'd heard it, they
didn't want us.

Henry Priestman, The Christians, 1987

**The one dilemma of living
here is giving so much money
to a government I disapprove
of. Every year there's another
cruise missile with my name
on it.**
George Michael, 1987

**The punks hated us for
Knebworth, and quite rightly
so. But we couldn't go
playing the Nottingham Boat
Club just to prove to people
in long overcoats that we
were okay.**
Robert Plant, Led Zeppelin, 1987

We won't go on Saturday
morning television any
more because they make
fools of you.

Neil Tennant, Pet Shop Boys, 1987

**We were victims of Seventies
self-indulgence.**
Kevin Godley, ex-10CC, 1987

*People want you to stay the way you were in 1971
just because that was when they were 20,
were having fun and weren't divorced yet.*

Loudon Wainwright III, 1987

Our songs are written in Icelandic and translated into English – and then re-translated into nonsense by the critics.

Björk, The Sugarcubes, 1987

I ate before Michael and I'll eat after Michael.

Frank Dileo, Michael Jackson's manager, 1987

If The Undertones had had the opportunity to sell out, they probably would have taken it.

Feargal Sharkey, 1987

In my opinion it's everyone else that's mad.

Mark E Smith, The Fall, 1987

My friendship with David Bowie seems to be over. I don't know what I've done to upset him, but when I turned up for a pre-arranged interview with him he just walked past me and said, 'You're a fat shit'.

Jonathan King, 1987 ▶

People wouldn't look twice at me if I wasn't in the pop charts.

Rick Astley, 1987

My wife left me because of the band and everything – but fuck it, I'd have left the bitch anyway.

Alec John Such, Bon Jovi, 1987

It's pretty dumb to write off CDs as belonging to yuppies. They should belong to everyone and the price should come down to a point where there are no social connotations involved.

Peter Gabriel, 1987

We're more rock'n'roll than Def Leppard. We're more rock'n'roll than anybody.
Pal Waktaar, A-Ha, 1987

....

It's terrible really, I even get bored with beautiful women, I've gone out with some extremely beautiful women and yet most of them are crushingly boring.
Terence Trent D'Arby, 1987

....

Take Whitney Houston – after a month of waking up next to her life would get very boring.
Terence Trent D'Arby, 1987

....

I could definitely challenge The Beastie Boys to a hotel room-smashing contest. I've been at it far too long for them, they're beginners.

When I hear Terence Trent D'Arby has smashed up a hotel room, I just think, 'Ha ha ha, that'll cost you!'
Rod Stewart, 1987

....

I'll always be able to scream on pitch. I'll always be able to scream wicked. And if they don't like it they can shove it.
Terence Trent D'Arby, 1987

....

Everybody dreams of getting hold of an autograph hunter and shouting 'WHY DON'T YOU LEAVE ME ALONE YOU LITTLE BASTARD!!!!'
Paul Heaton, The Housemartins, 1987

....

Bruce Springsteen? Oh, he's great, but he needs his hair styled.
James Brown, 1987

....

I can't understand why nobody else has realised that Michael and Janet Jackson are one and the same person.
Mick Jones, Big Audio Dynamite, 1987

I'd like to see him dead. I'd like to shoot him. He owns acres and acres of land, with big houses he's never seen. And there are people living in squalor in some of those places. I have no sympathy at all.

Ian Brown, Stone Roses, on Prince Charles, 1989

....

I try not to repeat myself. It's the hardest thing in the world to do – there are only so many notes one human being can master.

Prince, 1989

....

The Royal Family is unnecessary to attract tourists. In this country there has been history and the tradition which arouses people's interest as a basis. It's unfair that one individual owns so much private property and is living gracefully, don't you think? I should shut my mouth now, otherwise my name might be on the National Front blacklist.

Ian Brown, Stone Roses, 1989

....

I saw Sting on German TV and he looked really patronising, like a teacher. I think that could put people off issues like that, but I'll say what I think about anything. What do I think about the environment then? You should stop killing whales and dolphins, for a start.

Ian Brown, Stone Roses, 1989

....

Anyone who says they don't want to see their record in the chart is full of shit!

Lars Ulrich, Metallica, 1988

I'd like to kick the Queen out of Buckingham Palace and deny everyone that's supposed to be aristocratic their aristocratic rights; because I don't believe they should have them by birthright.

Bobby Gillespie, Primal Scream, 1990

Actually television is pretty crap, isn't it? I don't think we should watch it. I never watch television. Everything except *The Hitman And Her* is boring. And that's on at four in the morning. I watch it every week...

Neil Tennant, Pet Shop Boys, 1990 ◥

My bad habit, I guess, is a good habit nowadays. I can't tolerate a lot of bullshit and that makes me short tempered, I used to give everyone a chance but I'm not so sure nowadays, I think

you just get on with your own life and cut the crap. I also can't stand it when people aren't diligent and they're not putting maximum effort into things. It's such a waste of life.

Wendy James, Transvision Vamp, 1990

Neil: There's nothing about New Kids that interests me. I think it's because they sing about boring things.
Chris: They're not even good looking, that's what gets me.
Pet Shop Boys, 1990

Do I like the sound of my own voice? Ooooh, no, not at all. I never listen to myself on the radio. I'm too nasal. I mean, I've got used to it, but I don't listen back to my voice if I can possibly help it. It embarrasses me.

Steve Wright, DJ, 1990

....

Do I watch the Queen's Speech at Christmas? No. I'd rather have lighted matchsticks stuck under my toenails. I find the Royal Family offensive. They just rub British people's noses in the dirt by reminding them that they can't afford to go ski-ing every two weeks. I find it physically offensive to watch it.

Norman Cook, then of
Beats International, 1990 ◣

....

What I think is worrying is that they decided to create a law, which was not needed anyway, so once this whole 'rave' thing has died out there's still going to be a law.

Neil Tennant, Pet Shop Boys, 1990

....

You want to know the truth? It's comical. Every time I get a magazine that says Megadeth on the cover, that's the first thing I turn to. Let's see what Dave [Mustaine] has to say today. Let's see how he can put his size 11s in his mouth again. The funny thing about Dave is every time I see him it's, 'Oh Lars, I said some really bad things about you in some magazine and I'm sorry'. Dave! Fuck it! Relax! He's on an emotional roller coaster.

Lars Ulrich, Metallica, 1991

....

You think one day some fucker's gonna tell you, 'You have a Number One record in America' and the whole world will ejaculate. I stood there in my hotel room and there was this fax that said, 'You're Number One'. And it was like, 'Well, OK'. It was just another fucking fax from the office.

Lars Ulrich, Metallica, 1991 ◢

....

It makes me itch to think of myself as Captain Beefheart... I don't even have a boat.

Captain Beefheart, 1991

....

Most people out there have to bend over for a buck just to pay the rent or whatever, so it's horrible to see rock'n'roll stars doing it because they've got a shitload of dough anyway. It's just embarrassing to see someone wrap their arms around a Coke can and kiss it for money when they don't need the money. It's not a big deal... I mean people that provide your gear, your strings on your guitar, that's always happened. So, we don't want to get too sanctimonious about it. But it's just where you draw the line. Also, for young bands, I can't blame them, if they want to appear as a sponsored act and they have no money...

Bono, U2, 1992

....

I hate rehearsing, if I can get out of it in any way, I'll do it.

Lemmy, Motörhead, 1991

> *Bono's so absorbed win the idea of himself as almost messianic, and then he realised he looks a complete prat.*
>
> **Robert Smith, The Cure, 1993**

The whole idea of dangerous is still rooted in the Sixties. What was dangerous back then is not at all dangerous now. The whole thing, this self-destruct thing, the whole sex and drugs and rock and roll, that's playing into the hands of the corporations. They just call it built-in obsolescence, you know, burn out some rock'n'roll star, find another one. That's all bullshit.

Rebellion is a much more sophisticated thing now. To be subversive is not to smash up your hotel room – your record company will be very happy about that. You know if I wanted to piss in a BBC cup here that might be very good for record sales but it is not dangerous or rebellious. I actually cannot believe that people still fall for the old shite. It's too easy, I can't believe that people are still plugged into that idea.

Bono, U2, 1992

....

Things are paid for, people pick you up, everyone's really nice to you. We live in this little bubble which is not really a good representation of everyday life. It's incredible, we're pampered little babies. We're spoilt brats. So it's easy. We're rich pompous rock stars who stay in big fancy hotels and smoke cigars and drink wine...

Chad Smith, Red Hot Chili Peppers, 1992

....

The things of the spirit are what is really rebellious... that's what actually put people's noses out of joint right now and not sex. Sex... corporations are built on that, it sells Pepsis, sells Coca Colas, sells everything. We're shocked so easily, it's sad.
Bono, U2, 1992

The music press [are] kind of suddenly coming around. It's like when we brought 'Creep' out, it received a fairly indifferent review in *New Musical Express*. And then four months later, they were describing it as a classic single, as if they'd finally come around to liking it. It's very strange.
Jonny Greenwood, Radiohead, 1993

You can see it in fucking shopping malls in middle America now, flares and platforms. Six years ago everyone was laughing at me, saying what an asshole I was.
Lenny Kravitz, 1993

Famous people are the ultimate star fuckers, which is endearing in a way because it makes them human. Fame is indiscriminate, but once you're in the club it doesn't matter how you got there.
Michael Hutchence, INXS, 1993

We were there in the early days, making music while Jamiroquai was still taking his exams.
Brand New Heavies, 1993

I've still not learnt to master that Mariah Carey dog-whistle.
Lisa Stansfield, 1993

These bands that claim to be punk rock, they've just totally missed the point. They're all going on about The Clash and slogans and taking speed and all that, but they're all dead uptight about it. For me, punk rock was the Sex Pistols, and they were Big Time Fun. They covered the Small Faces and Chuck Berry and Johnny Rotten went on *Desert Island Discs* in 1977 and all he played was Neil Young…

Noel Gallagher, Oasis, 1994

Don't talk to me about Nirvana. He was a sad man who couldn't handle the fame. We're stronger than that. And you can fuck your fucking Pearl Jam.

Liam Gallagher, Oasis, 1994

'I fucking hate being here!

Miles Hunt, The Wonder Stuff, on tour in America, 1993

I live with the guy, and that's what he is. He's a fucking slob. Ask me Mam.

Noel Gallagher, Oasis, on Liam 1994

We've never destroyed a hotel or anything like that, cause it's always somebody's mum who'd got to go down on her fucking knees and clean up the shit for £1.50 an hour.

Bobby Gillespie, Primal Scream, 1993 ◥

I can't say *Top Of The Pops* was a programme I got a great deal out of compering – really you're just a bingo caller on there, there wasn't a great deal else to it. From the point of view of satisfaction in television terms, it didn't do a great

*I tell you, when I read that Oasis is
Noel's band, that really fuckin' sent me...
It's no-one's band. It's all of us.
Take one away and there's nowt left.*

Liam Gallagher, Oasis, 1994

deal for me, but it made me very well known. Personally, I get more out of appearing on the Noel Edmonds show now, I get more fun being gunged on the Noel Edmonds show than I did actually compering *Top Of The Pops*, because it's more of a show. With *Top Of The Pops* it was really just calling out numbers.

Tony Blackburn, ex-BBC DJ, 1994 ◥

....

I'm not a rock singer and I don't want to be a rock singer. I'm not interested. It doesn't seem to get across.

Van Morrison, 1994

....

I heard that your brain stops growing when you start doing drugs. Let's see, I guess that makes me 19.

Steven Tyler, Aerosmith, 1994

....

With the punk thing, everyone was making impractical attacks on being rich or having money, ya know, but they all wanted to be rich.

Boy George, 1994

....

The world seems a little bit short on revolution to me right now. There are a few bands out there, but on the whole it seems like the

I never believed that U2 wanted to save the whales. I don't believe that The Beastie Boys are ready to lay it down for Tibet.

Iggy Pop, 1994

> *Achievement is for the senators and scholars.*
> *At one time I had ambitions, but I had them*
> *removed by a doctor in Buffalo.*

Tom Waits, 1994

computer age is really the current revolution, and that doesn't flow well with my own natural tendency to gravitate toward organic expressions and actually do things with your hands and your feet and your body and your vocal cords and your fingers and stuff like that. That appeals to me more than sitting in a room with a screen. Even if you are creating art on a screen, personally I'd rather do it in the flesh.

Anthony Kiedis, Red Hot Chili Peppers, 1994 ◥

....

Destroy everything. That's all

well and fine, but you got to offer something in its place. Since I always have a point and purpose to what I do, that's why people accuse me of being calculated. It's the way I am. I always know my next move. I could never conjure up a death wish, this is all I have is life. I don't know what comes next, and frankly I'm in no rush to find out. I don't believe in playing a martyr just for the sheer hell of it. And for something as childish as rock'n'roll is not on.

John Lydon, 1995

....

I don't need a Rolls Royce, I don't need a house in the country, I don't want to have to live in France. I don't have any rock and roll heroes; they're all useless. The Stones and the Who don't mean anything anymore; they're established. The Stones are more of a business than a band.

John Lydon, 1995

....

Liam's got more stupid. When he was at school, he was quite normal. Now he's definitely mad. He's not mad like some people in bands are mad. He's madder than mad... He's just mad.

Noel Gallagher, Oasis, 1995

....

I was double rude to Justine [Frischmann] the other night going 'Go on and get your tits out'. It's her boyfriend innit, 'cos I love getting at 'im 'cos he's a dick. If anyone said that to my bird, I'd chin 'im. But I fancy her big style.

I'm having her, man. In the next six months it will be all over the press... I'll have been with her. Don't say it, though, 'cos I'm mad for her and that'll screw it right up.

Liam Gallagher, Oasis, 1995

....

They're a fucking mess, Blur are. They are the opposite from us. I mean, Elastica are better than them. I couldn't cope with that, me. No way would I allow my bird to be better than me, no way.

Liam Gallagher, Oasis, 1995

....

Lennon was probably a twat as a person. I probably wouldn't get on with him at all. In fact, I would probably have hated him but all I'm bothered about is his songs. Those songs meant a real lot to me. I don't care about songwriters, all I care about is the songs. So like, if I met Neil Young or Keith Richards or Mick Jagger tomorrow and they were really obnoxious and rude, I wouldn't stop listening to their music.

Noel Gallagher, Oasis, 1995 ▶

....

Oasis – they're a joke, aren't they? It's just lots of middle-class people applauding a bunch of guys who act stupid and write really primitive music and people say 'oh it's so honest'. It's just like the art world where they'll pick up on people outside the art world, on the periphery, and bring them in. The things they love about them are that they're out of their environment – they're working class, thick or mentally ill. It's a freak show – they're laughing at them but at the same time they can say 'look how wonderfully varied and cultural we are'.

Thom Yorke, Radiohead, 1995

....

There's this thing about a white rock band from England coming over and 'breaking' America – why should there be that weight put around every young band's neck?

Noel Gallagher, Oasis, 1995

....

It's not good to see the likes of Shed Seven in the charts. They're a shit little band, and they've had too much press. They're just a crap version of the Smiths, and that singer sounds like Björk. He's an idiot. It's like 'oh, all right, another crap indie band'. What's the point?

Liam Gallagher, Oasis, 1995

....

George Michael's been coming to loads of our gigs. And then there's people like Bono. He was at Earls Court, then I saw him again in Paris and he goes, 'All right, son.' I said, 'I'm not your son, mate.'

The American public really does want me to die. I'm not going to die.

Courtney Love, 1995

I mean, he's done a few good records, but what we're doing now pisses on U2. 'My son?' Fuck off.

Liam Gallagher, Oasis, 1995

We should have got even more awards really. There isn't another band in the country who can touch us. And they know it.

Liam Gallagher, Oasis, 1995

Would I accept an MBE? Yeah, I would because you could probably flog it. I'd accept but I'd rather he offered me a place in the fucking cabinet. Minister For Rock! They've got a Minister For Sport but who gives a fuck about sport, all that bollocks, running around in shorts and that! Fuck that nonsense! I could be the Minister For Rock. Just see myself in the House of Lords falling asleep and dribbling.

Noel Gallagher, Oasis, 1995

I think people tend to be negatively critical for the sake of it. And I find that a little bit tiresome, because, they've obviously just listened to the album once, and... I don't know... It's because it's Black Sabbath they think 'Black Sabbath, we must slag them off'. They don't really give it a listen, they don't listen to what's gone into it, or anything else. I mean, I'm not saying that everybody does, but you get such a lot... Particularly the

I didn't come all the way over [to America] to shake hands with some knobhead executive's wife.

Noel Gallagher, Oasis, 1995

rock-mags, just for the sake of it, they're gonna stick the knife in. Can't possibly say, 'Actually, I really like this record, this is really good', no, couldn't possibly do that, would be totally uncool... That's what annoys me. Journalism for the sake of it.

Cozy Powell, 1995

....

I see that Robert Plant and Jimmy Page are out on tour and The Rolling Stones are still playing and this becomes sad because if they've got nothing else to do with their lives then they have to go back into playing. I don't think they're doing it for money... I think basically they're so used to the attention, the applause, and that's not what it's supposed to be about.

Johnny Ramone, 1995 ◢

....

I'd be in the studio at one o'clock in the afternoon when we were supposed to start and Phil [Lynott] would turn up at midnight ready to go all night because he'd just had some coke. I can't be bothered to pretend that I'm enjoying it after a while, it's not my lifestyle.

There's this famous phrase from Jesse Owens, the black runner at Hitler's Olympic Games. When he was about 80 they took him back to Munich and asked him what he thought of Hitler now. He said 'Well, I's here and he ain't!' I suppose it's a bit like that, really. It's always sad but you choose your own path, don't you?

Snowy White, Thin Lizzy, 1995

....

I stopped reading the press when they printed I was

going to top myself. And my girlfriend rings me up really, really upset, saying, 'What's all this, what have you been saying?' You know, that's when I stopped reading it. That was enough for me... I'm in this business, but I also want to be in this business on my own terms, you know.

Thom Yorke, Radiohead, 1995

....

Look at the history of British bands. Most are from the middle class, with the stress on higher education. The young people turn to music as a reaction to the middle-class treadmill. They form their own little gangs.

Ed O'Brien, Radiohead, 1995

....

I thought that basically it was the British press that did it to Richey [Edwards of the Manic Street Preachers]. Full stop. Although I've got lots of friends who are journalists, the few who I think were basically responsible for him having a breakdown I will always hold responsible and I will always see what we do in that light... And I think he is still alive.

▶ Thom Yorke, Radiohead, 1995

....

I was very 'cheap' – that's the way I'd always worked. I came back, and started our production company, called Loose End Productions, with Peter Collins. I can't remember what the first record we ever did was now, but it went on to be a hit. Then we did things like Tracey Ullman, the Belle Stars, and all of that lot. Again, it was hugely successful, and, again, I hated every minute of it. Not that I hated every minute of it for any other reason than I was producing records for other people, for the artists they'd found, in the way they wanted them to be. That wasn't fulfilling for me.

Pete Waterman, 1995

....

The older you get, the longer you've been doing it, if you don't get on it starts to become... tedious. And it isn't gonna work. You're gonna say 'I don't wanna do this anymore, sod it', and so the band's gonna change. I think that's what happened with Sabbath when they tried to re-do the old line-up. The chemistry was just wrong, it was never gonna work, and the Ozzy-thing, that was never gonna work either. So my question is, why spoil something that's already good to regrow old grounds? It's pointless.

Cozy Powell, 1995

....

When people of my generation left school, they had only three choices offered them: football, music or the dole. That's why there are so many big rock groups from the North.

Noel Gallagher, Oasis, 1996

....

What do I think about the Brits committee? They're a bunch of twats who think people like Sting and Bowie are the cutting edge of music.

Noel Gallagher, Oasis, 1996, after picking up three awards

....

Elves and dragons and all that bollocks! Ronnie James Dio does what he does and he does it very well, so why not? I just don't do that. I never saw any fairies at the bottom of my fuckin' garden, they were all out front at the pub.

Lemmy, Motörhead, 1996

....

Them lot [tabloids], I think they fancy me. I think they're

Jazz is fucking shit. Jazz is fucking stupid.

Liam Gallagher, Oasis, 1997

all gay. That's what I think anyway.

Liam Gallagher, Oasis, 1997

....

Americans want grungey fucking people, stabbing themselves in the head on stage. They get a bright bunch like us, with deodorant on, they don't get it.

Liam Gallagher, Oasis, 1997

....

Knebworth was top, but I wouldn't do it again. There's too much flying about in fucking helicopters with those gigs. I don't like flying: it's fucking petrifying.

Noel Gallagher, Oasis, 1997

....

I find it bizarre that Tom Cruise, Nicole Kidman and Madonna are buying property [in London]. I hear you have Planet Hollywood. That's the embassy, that's why they're all moving over, they've got a refuge. To me, Jon Bon Jovi singing about Chelsea is the same thing as Mick Jagger singing about New York. I bet you Jagger had a blast in New York City in 1975 going into Central Park with a couple of Mexican women, a bottle of wine and Keef.

Dave Grohl, 1997

....

I hate people who are cruel. I don't care whether it's to animals or people – I can't stand it. I see it going on around me all the time and I tell you, it annoys me like mad.

Peter Andre, 1997

....

The Spice Girls are like heroin.
You know somebody's doin' it, but nobody
is willing to admit that it is them.

Stand-up comedian and actor Chris Rock, 1998

You can't go home with the Rock and Roll Hall of Fame. You don't sleep with the Rock and Roll Hall of Fame. You don't get hugged by the Rock and Roll Hall of Fame, and you don't have children with the Rock and Roll Hall of Fame. I want what everybody else wants: to love and to be loved, and to have a family. Being in love has always been the most important thing in my life.
Billy Joel, 1998 ◥

....

I was never an icon and I was also never a woman who acted in a political way. Of course, I fought against male domination, against a world ruled by men, but I never wanted to change the world and turn male domination into female domination. What I did I did for myself, to free myself. I never really planned to be an idol for millions of women all over the planet and I never saw men in general as the enemy. The enemies were people who tried to suppress me.
Madonna, 1998

....

If Bill Clinton can't get a blow job off his secretary then he's in the wrong job.

Ozzy Osbourne, 1998

Oasis are the Spice Girls in drag!
Geri Halliwell, Spice Girls, 1998

I have this strange feeling of being the only person so far who has left The Rolling Stones and is still alive.

Mick Taylor, 1998

....

I watched them drop their first Es. I was in Shoom in '89, watched them come in wearing their glittery gear and platform shoes, their rock 'n' roll gear. I was sat there laughing at them. I like their record collections – but that's about it.

Ian Brown, Stone Roses, on Primal Scream, 1998 ◥

....

What annoys the hell out of me is the arrogance of some people. They don't even listen to our music, they decided in advance that they don't like it. You know even before we finished the album, before anybody ever heard just one track, some people had decided that it will suck. I don't give a shit about them. If they can't appreciate good music, it's their own fault.

Billie Joe Armstrong, Green Day, 1998

....

Gary Barlow couldn't write 'Angels'. He couldn't write a song with such spiritual intent and actually mean it.

Robbie Willams, 1998

....

If someone is waiting for me to die, he can forget it. I'm already dead.

Iggy Pop, 1998

I just didn't want this kid telling me what I could or couldn't be. I'm not gonna turn to him and say, 'Oi mate, stop wearing eyeliner'.
Goldie on The Prodigy's Keith Flint, 1998

I would never consider getting my body pierced. Not my nipples, not my dick, not my tongue, nothing. When I get a new tattoo now I insist on new needles, new ink, the lot.
Ozzy Osbourne, 1998

I'd like to destroy rare items of Sex Pistols' memorabilia every week. Yes, I could sell them or give them all to charity, but it's more fun to burn them.
John Lydon, 1999

We only met Madonna once and she was acting like she knew us. Even she asked us why Geri had left. We said, 'None of your business, Madonna!'
Victoria Beckham, Spice Girls, 1999

I don't give a fuck if you think I'm crap.
Melanie Chisholm, ex-Spice Girls, to audience at V99, 1999

The boys can take of their shirts when they get hot, so why can't I?
Courtney Love, 1999

Girl Power in terms of Spice Girls seems to be more like, we can get our tits out whenever we want - which is basically what blokes want anyway!'
Jarvis Cocker, 1998

I hate people asking me what I mean in my songs, 'cause it's none of their business. I also hate being asked, 'How do I feel being a woman in rock.'

Sinead O'Connor, 1999

Keith Richards – there's no uglier man than him, but his hair makes him look sexy.
Rod Stewart, 1999

encores. What's with your writers? Your writers are fucking dicks.
Eminem and UK press, 1999

They were full of shit, these magazines and newspapers were full of shit. We performed for 40 minutes and one paper said it was only 20 and the other paper said it was 15 minutes. I only had one album's worth of material but we did two encores and performed for 40 minutes and so we did damn near every song on the fucking record, plus some freestyle shit and some

Your wife is probably sleeping with everyone while you're away.
Sinead O'Connor to Neil Finn, 1999

The most successful comeback thing was Kiss, wasn't it? But they're not Kiss like they were, you know? I mean, they might be better or worse, but they're not the same. You don't get the same vibe.
Lemmy, Motörhead, 1999

*Courtney's in her dressing room
playing with her dirty pussy.*

Marilyn Manson, 1999

The food is horrible, it fucking sucks. I don't know how you guys live over there [UK]. I can't see how there are fat people over there because I'd never want to eat. But other than that I like it, it's cool. I do think you guys are a little bit too polite, a little bit too nice.
Eminem, 1999 ◣

A desperate desire to get laid has driven my career. Ugly pop stars get laid. Ugly accountants don't.
Fatboy Slim, 1999

I told Shaun [Ryder] I'd work with the Mondays again. It's just he's got to realise when you go into a studio it helps to have songs!
Paul Oakenfold, producer/remixer, 1999

I was sitting on the crapper looking at the toilet paper; and I was thinking. 'How come there's no Kiss toilet paper out there?' There will be four different types so you can take a swipe with any one of us.
Gene Simmons, 1999

I didn't realise I still hated so many people.
Pete Wylie at Roger Eagle's Memorial service, 1999

He's a great singer – but he's not the most masculine guy, is he?
Alexander O'Neal speaking about Michael Jackson, 1999

*Tin Machine features the two worst lines
I've written, and there have been many.*

David Bowie, 1999

A Police reunion? He [Sting] wouldn't do a reunion unless I went on a rampage at all the shops and bankrupted him.

Trudie Styler, aka Mrs Sting, 1999

....

Thank God I didn't invent anything as banal as punk rock. It was basically something between high-school prom and pub rock.

Iggy Pop, 1999 ▶

....

I've heard that he's doing a Radio 3 play. Earth-shattering, isn't it! At least six listeners, I think.

Roger Daltrey on Pete Townshend, 1999

....

Marilyn Manson? Yeah, really original. Stick some make-up on and give yourself a girl's name. That's never been done.

Alice Cooper, 1999

....

We were all pals just having the best fucking time possible... by the end, I didn't talk to Rod except to say 'fuck you' on stage.

Ian McLagan (the Faces), 1999

....

I think it's better to end up in court arguing over money than winding up as smack addicts.

John Keeble, ex-Spandau Ballet, after losing royalty dispute to former colleague Gary Kemp, 1999

....

[They're] mostly drab little bank clerks who've had a result.

Ian Dury on today's rock gods, 1999

You don't have to write about killing little girls. If they're making all this money, let them write about something good in their lives.

Gary Rossington, Lynyrd Skynyrd, on Marilyn Manson, 1999

....

I think the best way to describe Teignmouth would be if we sent you the article that was printed on the front page of the local paper. There's a picture of the mayor of Teignmouth putting our CD in the bin because apparently we said in some interview that

Teignmouth is a boring place, full of drug-takers. He said 'I don't know who these drug-takers are, no-one takes drugs here...' Ha ha ha! That gives you an idea of what the town is like.

▶ Matt Bellamy, Muse, 1999

....

I've got to admire [Kate Bush] because Peter Gabriel tried to shag her and she wasn't having any. She's the only woman on Earth who ever resisted him, including me.

Sinead O'Connor, 1999

....

All a record company is is a bank, and they loan you a little money to make a record and then they own you for the rest of your life. You don't even own your own work.

Tom Waits, 1999

*I don't know how that rumour started
about him coming back to my apartment.
Everybody knows I like younger men.*

Madonna on Paul McCartney, 2000

Pavarotti's meant to have a great voice but I think he's shite. Rubbish. That's not singing.
Liam Gallagher, Oasis, 2000

If Britney is being called the new Madonna it's all right by me, but there's more to being Madonna than taking your clothes off.
Madonna, 2000

For somebody that is such a big supporter of freedom of speech, and for somebody that freely speaks his mind about what he thinks about pop music – acts such as 'N Sync, Britney Spears, whatever – you know, [Eminem] kind of took it too hard whenever I spoke my mind and had my freedom of speech about domestic violence, which was never even a diss towards him, which is I guess the reason why he put that song out in the first place, so I don't know. I guess he couldn't take it... whatever.

▼ Christina Aguilera, 2000

'NSync have become Andy Warhol's tomato-soup can. And I can buy into why people dig it.
Shirley Manson, Garbage, 2000

He said to me, 'There's only room for one face in the mirror. We can't both be doing this job and I was doing it first.'

Justine Frischmann on splitting with Damon Albarn, 2000

One day I'll be DJ-ing and getting a blow-job from Zoe and it'll be all too much... my brains will be all over the decks.

Fatboy Slim, 2000

I went home and fucked all their girlfriends. I'm a great believer in revenge.

◀ Lemmy on being kicked out of Hawkwind, 2000

I cannot believe how expensive real estate is here... I could get my mind around buying a house for $6 million in America and here, you get tricked into thinking £6 million is $6 million. It's just too outrageous and I'm just too middle-class to throw my hard-earned money away like that.

Madonna, 2000

I've met Britney [Spears] a couple of times but I'm not going to demolish her in public. I'm not a fan of her music because I think that the boy/girl bands are garbage. I think that shit is trash, it's as corny as fuck but whatever... let them do their thing. I can't knock her for doing her thing, she sucks and she can't sing but whatever.

Eminem, 2000

There are backing singers out there whose voices put us to shame, but they are not here, they don't have whatever it is.

Victoria Beckham, Spice Girls, 2000

Who's Tony Blair, did he get his dick sucked?

Eminem, 2000

Christina Aguilera's been on MTV, talking about my personal fuckin' business... I got married, that's my personal fuckin' business! [adopts high-pitched voice] 'I think he's married, yeah, and doesn't he have this song about killing his baby's mother and stuffin' her in the trunk? Y'know, I always tell my friends, domestic violence and blah blah.'

That song was not meant to be taken seriously, that song was my sick, psychotic thoughts, 'cos she doesn't know what was goin' on in my personal life when I wrote that song, my daughter was being kept from me, but what she doesn't know, what the giggly little girl doesn't know, is that the same girl that I said I stuffed in a fuckin' trunk I married! I married her. So she was running her mouth and not knowing the fuckin' facts.

Eminem, 2000

People today are still living off the table scraps of the sixties.

Bob Dylan, 2000

I fucking hate Europe in bold letters with exclamation points!

Eminem, 2000

I spend more time in America, but it's only while my kids go to school. As soon as they're done, I'm out of here like a bat out of hell. The weather's nice in LA but you can't beat a good plate of fish and chips.

Ozzy Osbourne, 2000

Metallica have turned into a bunch of fucking corporate pigs. You sold out to your record company and lawyers with this lawsuit. In fact, you sold out years ago. Suck my dick.

Nikki Sixx, Mötley Crüe, 2000

I have a bone to pick with Queensryche. We had a summer tour being booked with those guys – but they backed out at the 11th hour which fucked us over. Maybe they realised that having to play after us would make their fans realise how much they suck now!

Mike Portnoy, Dream Theater, 2000

There are quite a few honest songwriters out there writing about relationships and their own personality traits. But for some reason, once they step out of the bedroom, their honesty doesn't seem to come with them.

Billy Bragg, 2000

I can piss and shit in front of anybody. Being in a band you have to learn to, because sometimes you don't have a choice.

Shirley Manson, 2000

I believe he's now working on Volume II, ransacking my dustbin for clues to lesbianism.

Morrissey on biographer Johnny Rogan, 2000

They don't have to downgrade women and use profanity, and they shouldn't make a record they can't take home to their mother.

James Brown with advice to rappers, 2000 ▼

....

I once sat next to Michael Bolton and said, 'Have you thought about getting your hair cut?' Yasmin kicked me so fucking hard.
Simon Le Bon, Duran Duran, 2000

....

I'm a big mouth – whatever happens I'll look like a big-mouth bitch.
Sharon Osbourne, 2000

....

I was very good friends with Elvis, you know. He lived in Palm Springs, had a house here and was here a lot. We spent a lot of time together here and in Las Vegas. I was at one end of the house doing drugs and he was at the other end of the house doing drugs and neither of us knew – I'm serious!

John Phillips, The Mamas & The Papas, 2000

....

I don't know if you ever saw *Spinal Tap*, but that was my life! In fact the last tour we did we called the Spinal Tubes Tour cos it was a disaster. Somebody's

Had I been in charge of Elvis, instead of Tom Parker, he would still have been alive today.

Sam Phillips, Sun Records, 2000

*Spirituality and celibacy do not go hand in hand.
Far from it!*

Sinead O'Connor's view on the Catholic faith, 2000

girlfriend took over as manager after I left, just like *Spinal Tap*, so when I came back they had this girl who didn't know what she was doing, didn't have a clue. We got rid of her and for the last three or four years I was the manager. People don't want to talk to artists – record companies, booking agents and accountants assume the artist is a fuckin' idiot and doesn't know what the fuck they're doing! Who's the manager? *I'm* the manager! Oh, *really*?
Fee Waybill, Tubes, 2000

Walter [Becker] has an aura that suggests if you fucked with him he would go to the ends of the earth to get even. This has been very good for Steely Dan.
Donald Fagen, Steely Dan, 2000

Everything has gone wrong in my life and I blame it on Phil Collins. He told me I should buy this computer but after 18 months of going plink plonk I lost half the tracks.
◀ John Martyn, 2000

I've heard the Backstreet Boys and Britney Spears... My 15-year-old girl wouldn't be caught listening to those things.
Neil Young, 2000

I might as well quit now, – that's bollocks!

**Gary Numan at the idea of
William (Star Trek) Shatner covering 'Cars', 2000**

It certainly isn't art. Sticking pieces of paper on things goes back to potty training... messing about with your own shit. Stop it now. Go back to singing, if that's what he calls it.

Critic Brian Sewell on Robbie Williams' first work of art, 2000

The song ['Trouble'] is about behaving badly towards somebody you really love and I was certainly doing that to some members of the band. I suppose it's about a time when I was being a bit of a knobhead.

Chris Martin, Coldplay, 2000

Oh my God, he looks like Stephen King! The pee stripe on the side of his head is never nice. And he's wearing girly trainers and tighty jeans to show off his wad! The ugliest yet.

Daphne, Daphne & Celeste, on the Charlatans' Tim Burgess, 2000 ◀

The middle-class thing has never been relevant. We live in Oxford, and in Oxford we're fucking lower class. The place is full of the most obnoxious, self-indulgent, self-righteous oiks on the fucking planet, and for us to be called middle class... well, no, actually. Be around

I've always wanted to smash a guitar over someone's head. You just can't do that with a piano.

Elton John, 2000

> *You see blokes like Craig David meet a girl on Monday and make love by Wednesday. What's the delay? Craig needs to work on his approach.*
>
> **Derek Smalls, *Spinal Tap*, 2000**

on May Day when they all reel out of the pubs at five in the morning puking up and going 'haw haw haw' and trying to hassle your girlfriend...

Thom Yorke, Radiohead, 2000

....

I'm a champagne socialist, apparently. Someone called me that last night; I got into a massive row with this guy.

Thom Yorke, Radiohead, 2000

....

I'd find Phil Collins and kick him in the balls all day long.

Trey Parker, South Park creator, on his 'perfect day', 2000

....

Thom [Yorke]'s got quite a legacy with the music press. I think in 1995 his face was on the cover of a magazine with the words: 'Is this going to be the next rock'n'roll suicide?' Why do you think he doesn't want to talk to people? I think he's got better things to do with this time.

▼ Ed O'Brien, Radiohead, 2000

....

He's [Liam] getting on my fucking nerves at the moment. I hate not being able to go to my own studio because he won't sing when I'm there because it freaks him out. It's just like fuck off. You know, either sing or don't sing, but don't do some fucking pastiche of the two. 'I think I might sing today, but I think I'm not in a good mood.' It's like, who do you think you are? Jim Morrison? You're meant to be an untortured artist. Either shit or get off the bog, man.

Noel Gallagher, Oasis, 2001

....

Liam thinks he's the new John Lennon. He thinks he's fantastic. But who's gonna tell him? The same way, who's going to say to me that maybe a song's not going to be good enough?

Noel Gallagher, Oasis, 2001

....

I've never been one for donating large amounts of money to charity because I donate a lot of money as it is. It's called forty fucking-per-cent tax.

Noel Gallagher, Oasis, 2001

....

Walking through the doors at 10 Downing Street, not as a plumber but an invited guest. I'm glad I did it to have a look, but in terms of New Labour, I recognise now that we were conned. We thought Blair was John F Kennedy, when in fact he was John Major with a better PR team!

Noel Gallagher, Oasis, 2001

....

You want to be thought of as attractive, but it's a competitive world and there's always going to be another beautiful girl around the corner... men are allowed

That bald cunt wants to get a wig.

Liam Gallagher on Damon Albarn, 2001

> *The music scene at the moment if dominated by all that terrible teenage stuff.*
>
> **Thom Yorke, Radiohead, 2001**

not to meet the conventional standards of beauty.

Madonna, 2001

....

We don't have to sing anything we don't want to sing. If we don't like it we don't do it – it's as simple as that. Same with the image. We discuss what we like and the stylist works round that.

Kym Marsh, Hear'say, 2001 ◄

....

The stuff they do is disgusting, glamorising all the bullshit, lifestyle and peripheral crap. Hardly anything is about music.

Patti Smith on VH-2 and MTV, 2001

What a phoney! Working-class hero? My arse! He was about as working class as a Wilmslow dentist, that's why the tosser was at art school in the fifties. He wasn't sexy in the least – he was hideous, even when young.

Julie Burchill on John Lennon, 2001

....

The critics go on about our looks our training, what we're eating. They just won't focus on our singing. We worked so hard to get the sound together, to get our voices out there. Looks? Clothes? The criticism has to be about music, surely?

Myleene Klass, Hear'say, 2001

....

Where the hell is that place?
Who would travel 16 hours to get there?

Britney Spears on Australia, 2001

In the Sixties it was 23-year olds trying to sound grown up. Now you get 33 year-olds trying to be 18.

Chrissie Hynde, Pretenders, 2001

I think it's disgusting that bands like A1, Steps and Westlife get to Number 1. It's all crap.
Mel C, ex-Spice Girls, 2001

If it's true Geri Halliwell charged a fee, then that's a very bad show.
Dame Vera Lynn on Geri charging to entertain 'our boys' in Oman, 2001

I don't watch any porn films because it's like watching a geezer cook a steak when you're starving hungry. It frustrates me. I don't think girls are throwing themselves around as much as they used to. Or let's just say they aren't going the whole way like they did in my day.
Rod Stewart, 2001

I couldn't think of anything worse than a big cock up my arse-hole, quite honestly.
◀ Rod Stewart on same-gender sex, 2001

If The Beatles hadn't been good that name would have sounded stupid.
Fred Durst, Limp Bizkit, 2001

I heard Hugh Grant is supposedly a good footballer, which I don't

believe. Another thing I heard, just now actually, is that Stallone puts his own pictures on the wall whenever he checks into a hotel, which is unbelievable. I mean, I've a got a few at home of me playing football, but I wouldn't walk around with them in my suitcase and put them up in hotel rooms.

Rod Stewart, 2001

....

I don't listen to anything, and I don't read the papers, and I don't watch TV, and I don't go to concerts.

George Harrison, 2001

....

John Cale, you know him? I'm glad you do, because I didn't until I was supposed to have met him. He wrote something about me that was completely untrue, so I sued him. I won't go into what it was because I don't think he deserves the time of day. But it was utter nonsense, so I sued him and got money from him which I gave to charity, by the way.

▲ Bonnie Tyler, 2001

....

Bill Clinton's attempts to be friends with young people... did something to the rebellion barometer. It didn't

If everyone who was nasty to us rotted in Hell, it would be very crowded.

Yoko Ono, 2001

give kids any authority to go against. I think that's why there's been a lot of bland and happy-go-lucky music created over the past six or seven years. I didn't really support Bush, but I hope we get some good right-wing, Manson-hating people in office so I can piss them off.

Marilyn Manson, 2001

I'm still very presentable but I can't keep up with Mick [Jagger]. He has an unbelievably small backside and that's what women go for.

Rod Stewart, 2001

I used to tell Mick [Mars] that I wouldn't fuck her with his dick. She just seemed weird and misshapen, like someone had beat her face in with an ugly stick, albeit a very expensive ugly stick.

◀ Nikki Sixx, Mötley Crüe, on Pamela Anderson, 2001

I've never met a Beatle. I've flown with Paul McCartney but I didn't want to impose because I would have felt like a dickhead. He was with Linda and they didn't come near me because of, you know, the bat thing.

Ozzy Osbourne, 2001

How does he do it? I mean, he's older than me, and my ass is still really tight.

Iggy Pop on Mick Jagger, 2001

He's very pretty.
Maybe that's why he's so paranoid.

Boy George on Eminem, 2001

I fuckin' hate Xmas. It's the biggest wind up joke and waste of fucking money on the plant. 'There's only 175 shopping days left to Xmas'n'all that – oh fuck off! All that cooked bastard turkey and soggy Brussels sprouts, ah fuck no, I can't stand it.

Ozzy Osbourne, 2001

One thing that I've noticed about modern bands is that they don't seem to cultivate a unique, identifiable sound. Nobody does solos and nobody expresses themselves in that way.

Ozzy Osbourne, 2001

[Singer] Vince [Neil] had grown so fucking big since I last saw him that he looked like Roseanne Barr or something. His head was the size of a balloon and folds of fat were billowing over his watch. His body was a weird yellowy shade of brown that was probably a combination of liver problems from alcohol and sunburn from lazing around all day.

▲ Tommy Lee, Mötley Crüe, 2001

Colonel Gadaffi is madder than I am. He should stop fucking around with guns and buy a guitar. He'd be

87

the greatest rock star in the world.

Ozzy Osbourne, 2001

He was always mad. It was just something we got used to.

Leah Wood, Ronnie's daughter, on growing up with Uncle Keith, 2001

I say to all my guitar players, 'I want you to play a riff that will make a kid out there want to be the next Jimmy Page. Don't sound like fucking Steve Howe from Yes, or do all that finger tapping like Eddie Van Halen!'

Ozzy Osbourne, 2001

Did you ever meet Betty Ford? Yeah. I met her a couple of times. She was a very quiet lady. She'd come in like royalty, have the unit polished. She was all right,

though. She'd hover like a blow-up doll at one end of the wing and then go out the other. It was, like, 13 'Hail Bettys', and she'd go home.

Ozzy Osbourne, 2001

When I go on stage I'm friends with all these people [Marilyn Manson, etc], but my idea is never go up on stage if you don't think you can blow all these people off the stage. So that's maybe why I don't get old and fat and stupid and slow (laughs).

▲ Alice Cooper, 2001

We were in the Sony music offices the other day and it was all 'so and so is in the building today so can you not walk in the corridors? Huh? Michael [Jackson]'s here, is he? And I can't look at him in

the face? Wanna fucking bet?
I'll show him me fucking arse
before I look him in the eye if
you prefer!

Ozzy Osbourne, 2001

....

The Rolling Stones said
that the main
reason they got
into music was
to meet
women – what
a bunch of
wankers! We got
into music because
we loved music.

Bruce Dickinson, Iron Maiden, 2001 ▲

....

I'd like to stop the 'industry'
part of music industry
because right now there is a
manufactured line of
marketable pop boy and girl
bands – 'nice-tits-puckered

lips-keep the money
rolling in'. It's a fucking
assembly line!

Ozzy Osbourne, 2001

....

**Puff Daddy tried to attack
one of the guys from
Boyzone? Man, I'd
have paid a
hundred bucks
to have been
at ringside for
that fight! (I
blame Puff
Daddy] for the
decline of music in
the Nineties. He is the true
anti-Christ because he has
destroyed everything that is
good about rock'n'roll.**

Marilyn Manson, 2001

....

It seemed like there was
going to be a dispute

Oh, who gives a fuck?

Dave Gilmour on when the next Floyd album
is due to come out, 2001

I would rather have my testicles eaten by Hannibal Lecter than tour with Mötley Crüe again.

Dave Mustaine, Megadeth, 2001

between Moby and I, but it was all the fault of the media. They took an old quote of his and I assumed it was recent so I stood my ground and let him know he would receive a severe ass-whipping if he needed one. But he just sort of cowered in fear and went back to eating vegetables...

Marilyn Manson, 2001

....

I said fuck. It was their fault. They asked me!

Slash explaining why he swore on children's TV show CD:UK, 2001

....

Gene Simmons was an asshole. [Kiss] asked us to be on tour with them when they were trying to come back, then they told the press that

we were a corporate rock band. They should talk, with all the dolls and merchandise.

Jack Russell, Great White, 2001

....

In the Seventies there were some really horrible journalists, I suppose there still are, they are just more cynical now rather than deliberately horrible, yes definitely. I remember I closed a radio station down in Boston once! I called a DJ a cunt over the air, they didn't like that and they closed the station down.

Dave Davies, The Kinks, 2001

....

MTV does very little, MTV is essentially R&B and dance unfortunately. Not that there's anything wrong with

> *I made a dreadful mistake once of buying Mariah Carey's first album, because of the single it was a lovely bluesy track, but the rest of it was a complete nonsense.*
>
> **Midge Ure, 2001**

that, but there's no variation, it's too much of one kind of music. Everything else is squeezed into 2am slots for one hour. Radio 1 doesn't play anything at all vaguely interesting: there will always be exceptions, but it's Steps, Bewitched, Atomic Bollix type rubbish which is all very well. Again I'm not knocking it for what it is, but the thing I've always been upset about mainstream radio and TV is the lack of variety they give you. I don't mind them playing whatever they play, but instead of playing Spice Girls 15 times a day play it seven or eight times: you're still giving it exposure but you free up seven or eight slots for something else.

◀ Gary Numan, 2001

I should have been rude to [journalist] Jon Landau if I'd met him when he did the famous *Rolling Stone* Cream article – I should punched him in the hooter!

Jack Bruce, Cream, 2001

I saw it [the Greatest Eighties Tour Ever starring Bananarama, Kim Wilde and

Heaven 17] in the paper. I like [Heaven 17's] Glenn Gregory, he's one of my best pals, but it's not the sort of thing I want to do, those retro things. You could take the heads off those people and stick on Gerry & The Pacemakers, Freddie & The Dreamers – it's the same thing, and I don't want to go down that route.

Midge Ure, ex-Ultravox, 2001 ▲

....

Keyboard players tend to be lazy. Any manufacturer will tell you that when instruments come back to the shop for part exchange or whatever, 99 per cent of them still have all the original factory pre-sets in them.

Rick Wakeman, 2001

....

I was cleaning my teeth the other day and 'Eve Of Destruction' came on the radio. It's an awful song and that came about because of all the wonderful stuff Bob Dylan was writing. To write off Bob Dylan because of 'Eve Of Destruction' is mad and to write off the genuinely exciting energetic [progressive rock] because of all the dross of the bandwagon-jumpers... That 70 per cent of it was Spinal Tap doesn't take away from the fact that 30 per cent was inspiring stuff, people playing well and pushing at so many boundaries.

Rod Argent, 2001

....

I have been slagged off in my time! I remember one particular review I had in *Sounds* after the 'Circus' concert we did at the Roundhouse in Chalk Farm.

It was a very successful concert but the management neglected to give out free tickets to journalists – and one took this to heart so much that I happen to know he was in the bar rather than in the hall. He gave us a review in *Sounds* that began in capital letters 'Sod off, Rod Argent – you ain't that good!' I was incredulous, but in the end I think it did more good than harm. The next week there were all these letters from people asking what he was on about!

Rod Argent, 2001

....

I'm not saying English women are ugly, but the last time I played Hammersmith Odeon I looked out there in the front row and I thought the pig season had opened.

Ted Nugent, 2001

....

For some reason [Stereophonics'] Kelly Jones decided to say he did offer us a gig and we turned it down. He mentioned figures of money... I don't know what he is talking about. We've met him a few times and I thought he was a cool guy and got on with him. I don't know why he's currently started slagging us off. I'm just a little bit shocked by all that.

▲ Matt Bellamy, Muse, 2001

....

Manowar said that they were the loudest band in the world, but they probably got that record in the studio with a digital machine, so it's probably bollocks. Like the rest of their stage act.

Lemmy, Motörhead, 2001

....

I like to work quick, I hate to be laboured. When we were

It's about time we sold 10 million records.
I need another airplane.

Alex James, Blur, 2001

Meg and Patsy didn't get on.
It was a vicious nightmare.

Noel Gallagher, 2001

doing 'Last Temptation' we
wrote the album, went in
the studio, did the
tracks and did the
vocals in the
same time it
took for
Metallica to get
the drum sound
on their album!
One of the roadies,
Metallica's drum tech, came
in and said well we just got
the drum sound and I said
well how long did that take?
He said three months and
I said hey wait a minute, we
just did a whole album in
that time! I think some
people get really carried
away in the studio.

Alice Cooper, 2001

I have this kind of both
respect and loathing
of music journalists
because they're
trying
to put
something
into words
which
ultimately
is not decipherable.
That's why it's music. Then
on the flip side you can
destroy something that
someone's put a lot of soul
and effort into with one
article. It's so fickle. If
someone at, say *New Musical
Express* likes this band they're
made – forget about them if
the *NME* hates them.

▲ Will Champion, Coldplay, 2001

This is for everyone out there who's done Ecstasy... you fucking sad wankers.

Badly Drawn Boy, 2001

In the Seventies I looked like a walking tumbleweed! It's pretty fucking funny. It wasn't until I chopped all my hair off that I started looking halfway human.

Neal Schon, Journey, 2001

There's an inherent laziness in white British males – they don't want to get off their arses and work like Asian people.

James Walsh, Starsailor, 2001

We have no interest in an Eighties nostalgia trip. That was my least favourite decade. Reliving old glories? Soft Cell were anything but glorious.

Marc Almond, 2001 ◣

The truth is, I'm a tosser away from music.

Chris Martin, Coldplay, 2001

Bruce [Springsteen] never said if he liked our version of 'Blinded By The Light'. I actually asked him directly once and he changed the subject – I don't think he liked it at all. I know that he hated the Pointer Sisters' 'Fire'. I think he just probably found it a complete and utter bastardisation of his work because he's pretty precious

I know stuff about MI5 that'd shit your brain. But I can't tell you 'cos they'll do it to me too.

Thom Yorke, Radiohead, 2001

He's greedy and ridiculous.

Chuck D on Lars Ulrich, 2001

about his work – and quite rightly so, I suppose!

Chris Thompson, Manfred Mann's Earth Band, 2001

....

I thought it sucked. What a piece of shit. But it was a hit, and you've gotta love that.

Stewart Copeland on Puff Daddy's cover of the Police's 'Every Breath You Take', 2001

....

Our 'Waiting' video was totally a failure. MTV doesn't show any videos anymore. If we had a booty video – if we had girls shaking their ass in the video – it would probably get played. Actually, I am just really bitter right now.

Billie Joe Armstrong, Green Day, 2001

....

I've started to act like Bono I've even started to address the audience in a pseudo-American accent.

Badly Drawn Boy, 2001

....

If being smart enough to take over the business aspect of our band is perceived as anti-rock, then guess what? Go fuck yourself.

◄ Jon Bon Jovi, 2001

....

I only joined a band with three other people... There were no wives, family, pets, psychics, gurus, managers, agents, or any such thing.

David Lee Roth on why there will be no reunion with Van Halen, 2001

....

I've heard what they did and it's rubbish.

John Deacon, Queen, on his band mates' new recording of 'We Are The Champions' with Robbie Williams, 2001

Everyone's going on about The Strokes, but for me they're a bit retrogressive.

Sir Elton John, 2001

The radio makes hideous sounds.

Bob Dylan on modern music, 2001

I am really sick and tired of having to ask people who are younger than me whether I can do things. I didn't mind so much when I was in my twenties, I could pretend it was like being back in school. But it's gone on too long.

Robert Smith, The Cure, 2001 ◥

I would love to see the day when I could go into a record shop and ask, 'Could I buy a record that has not been made by a homosexual?'

PJ Proby, 2001

There are many dying children out there whose last wish is to meet me.

David Hasselhoff, singer/actor, 2001

How annoying to be performing on the first night and having an audience full of people with no talent there to judge you!

Mark Lamarr, DJ, 2001

Pick a note and sit on it for a while, ok?

Billy Joel offers advice to Christina Aguilera, 2001

*They come across like a bunch of cocks –
all walking around in parkas and big
sunglasses like they're fuckin' rock stars.*

Kelly Jones, Stereophonics, on Hear'Say, 2001

I just nodded and hoped they'd go away...

Liv Tyler on meeting the Gallaghers, 2002

Everyone in England has slagged [Swept Away] off without seeing it. Don't you think that's absurd? But I think the knives were going to come out for Guy anyway, even if he hadn't ended up with me. He had too much success with his first few films. That's how the media is: eventually they have to pull you down.
Madonna, 2002

Paul McCartney tries to be Mr Nice Guy with those little arched eyebrows. You want to go: 'Fuck Off. Get in the real world.'
Sharon Osbourne, 2002

If I have a party on tour I'm not grabbing for a Radiohead CD. Anybody who is grabbing for it isn't going to get laid, unless you're looking for a sympathy fuck.
▲ Kid Rock, 2002

He's a schmuck; he'll always be a schmuck. End of story.
Tracii Guns on Axl Rose, 2002

They don't play so much of me on the radio any more. I'm not worried, I've had a fair crack of the whip. Anyone who complains about it, like Status Quo and all them – pah, moaning on about it – it's pretty greedy.

They should do something different. Like me.

Rod Stewart, 2002

....

Simon Cowell is a dreadful piece of crap who drags the music business down whenever he rears his ugly head.

Roger Daltrey, The Who, 2002

....

My big hair was funny as fuck. I've got even gayer photos of the big hair, before Ozzy.

Zakk Wylde, 2002

....

When you fucking do Pantera riffs and rap over the top of it, and jump up and down, you're not going to impress me with that. A band like Creed, to me, needs to be

taken to fucking court and sued over their blatant, pathetic Goddam robbery of Pearl Jam.

Phil Anselmo, Pantera, 2002

....

I swear 100 per cent on a stack of Bibles that you will not see me with those clowns. Why would I throw those guys a life saver? You will see a reunited Kid Wicked before you see a reunited Skid Row.

Sebastian Bach, ex-Skid Row, 2002

....

I couldn't stand Janis Joplin's voice... She was just a screaming little loudmouthed chick.

Arthur Lee, Love, on Janis Joplin, 2002

....

There's some good people out there, but there's a lot of fluff too. Things like 'NSync and Britney these people are about as deep as a bird bath.

David Crosby, 2002

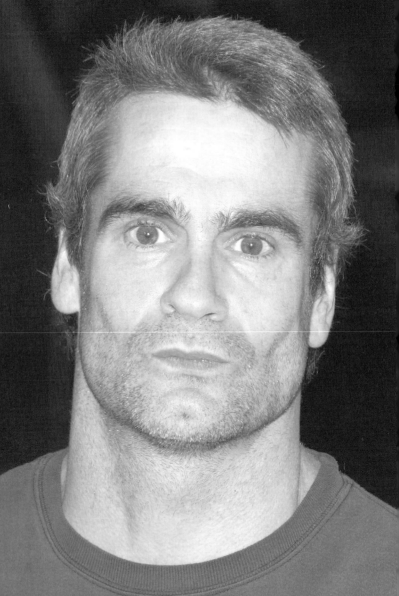

The only thing that gets in the way of music is musicians and their ego trips.

Henry Rollins, 2002

> The understanding of my art is only the sad product of journalism. Fuck art. I am art.
>
> Marilyn Manson, 2002

Certain radio programmes in America are always wondering why we just won't write the next 'Plush' or the next 'Interstate Love Song.' Y'know what? I got no fuckin' interest! If you wanna hear 'Plush' or 'Interstate Love Song', go buy a goddamned Creed record.

Scott Weiland, Stone Temple Pilots, 2002

If I'm as big as a house, maybe I should start charging rent. Some pussy ass writer at *NME* owes me rent – for living in my ass.

W Axl Rose, Guns N'Roses, 2002

If you ever run into Dave Grohl, I'm gonna kick his fuckin' arse. Because I think he sucks, and he wrote this cheese-dick song for Ozzy that I have to fuckin' play on… Foo Fighters is a fuckin' candyass girl band, but you've got that motherfucker submitting songs, and those douche bags from the Offspring submitted songs, too. I mean, none of these guys could play a Randy Rhodes solo if they tried. Dave Grohl? Fuck Dave Grohl! Let him get up there and play 'Mr Crowley'; he can't fuckin' do it. And it's like, you're getting this guy to write songs for Ozzy? Just because he played drums for fucking Shitvana?

▲ Zakk Wilde, 2002

105

To tell the truth, I've only listened to ['Live Era '87-93'] once. That record has a very sour note with me because my credit is horrible. When the record came out in '99 – and I play guitar on 90 per cent of it – the credit read 'additional musician'. I don't think it was cool for me and I don't think it was cool for the fans who went to those shows. They don't care if some of us don't get along or anything, they just want to hear good music, and that's so frustrating.

Gilby Clarke, ex-Guns N'Roses, 2002

Anthrax, stop ruining the name. Everybody is laughing at you guys. Honestly. I'm on the outside looking in. There was only one Anthrax. You guys are not Dave Mustaine, haven't you figured that out yet? Or should someone hit you with a brick?

Dan Spitz, ex-Anthrax, 2002

I told Blur they could remain jealous of my achievements and how many records I'd sold, or see sense and realise how much groundwork I've done for the next Blur LP. They know which side their bread's buttered.

Damon Albarn, the Gorillaz [and Blur!], 2002

All of a sudden I'm diagnosed manic-depressive – 'Lets put Axl on medication.' Well, the medication doesn't help me deal with the stress. The only thing it does is keep people off my back.

W Axl Rose, Guns N'Roses, 2002

My leaving of the band, I believe, was right before we really did the [Slash's] Snakepit record; right when my album was coming out. It happened pretty quick, but I don't have any regrets. I wouldn't change my decision. It was a strange thing: I'm

I did see Jordan close up once and she's actually really pretty, except for those great big tits.

Kelly Osbourne, 2003

telling Axl I don't want to be in the band any more and he's telling Slash on the other line he doesn't want me in the band! It was one of those unfortunate things. I can't change the way the guy feels, I don't have any regrets.

Gilby Clarke, ex-Guns N'Roses, 2002

....

I'm never eating another piece of fucking fish again. I went to stay at Elton John's in the South of France with Mum and Jack. We had dinner and we had shellfish. I spent the next two days with the shits and throwing up everywhere.

Kelly Osbourne, 2003

....

The women you see in videos are always stick figures. It's such a taboo to have women with rolls of flesh on them, but to me, they're so beautiful and strong. When you sit down you have a fat roll even if you're not fat. My six-year-old daughter has a fat roll. I feel very consoled by that. It's cool.

Madonna, 2003

....

Do you know I had to leave the red carpet when Christina Aguilera came down as she refused to do the red carpet while I was there? I think she's just a bit of a cow.

Kelly Osbourne at 2003 MTV Europe Awards

....

There have been plenty of times Noel (Gallagher) has said things about me in the papers and I've wanted to say something back, but then I think, No, keep your dignity.

Meg Mathews, ex-Mrs Gallagher, 2003

She's a fucking toothpick, she's a tart!

Kelly Osbourne on Christina Aguilera, 2003

Kelly really, really has got a dense head. I like Kelly, sister-wise. I think she has the ability to do great things in life but right now all she's concerned about is who her friends are and what to wear and she has no responsibilities at all. She's just like a stick in the wind and that could be a real big decline for Kelly. I mean, she could just ruin herself just by the way she's acting now. Because she's just always out at clubs. Never, never gives it a rest.

Jack Osbourne, 2003 ▲

....

[The paparazzi] are usually waiting at the end of the block. It's pretty irritating. But you know, what are you going to do? I complain about it, still nothing changes. I try to wear the same outfit all the time. I try to be really boring and have a really bland expression on my face, but it doesn't seem... I think they're waiting for me to fall off my bike or something. I don't feel like a prisoner. But do I get annoyed that I can't go for a bike ride or a walk without people following me? Yeah, I do.

Madonna, 2003

....

The critics have been writing

109

*I suppose people will call me Sir Mick,
but Sir Michael has a nice ring to it.*

Mick Jagger, 2003

me off for 20 years. That's nothing new. As far as I know I still have plenty of fans and sell a lot of records. Do I care what the critics say? No.

Madonna, 2003

It's nothing new. Keith likes to make a fuss. He's like a bawling child who has not got an ice cream. I think he would probably like to get one [knighthood] himself.

Sir Mick Jagger on Keith Richards, 2003

It's time for Eminem to go. He's a fucking sexist. He's not good for my fucking daughter. I want a good world for my daughter. When I saw 'It's so boring without me' in that song ['Without Me'], I just figured he'd written a nice song about me!

◀ Courtney Love, 2003

If [Richard] Branson's here he's going to get a smack in the mouth.

Air-rage suspect Courtney Love at an East London party, 2003

I was going to give her a little slap on the bottom for being a bad girl but I started chatting to her and we really hit it off.

Airline owner Richard Branson on Courtney Love, 2003

He (Paul McCartney)… has a knighthood, a wonderful little honour to be bestowed on one. I don't know why I haven't got any honour. I do my bit for charity.

Rod Stewart, 2003

He's pushing his face in all the time, telling us about his private life. Nobody's interested, he's incredibly rich, he should just go away.

Morrissey on Elton John, 2003

Christina [Aguilera]'s body is minging!
Kelly Osbourne, 2003

I wish my dad was still alive. He could fix those [Osbourne] kids in one night. I'd say 'Dad, could you fix those assholes for me? Thank you very much.'
Ted Nugent, 2003 ▲

Newspapers are full of lies, I don't want to have anything to do with them. It's just a rule in our house – nobody can bring magazines or newspapers into the house.
Madonna, 2003

Sharon Osbourne? Loved her like a mum, [but] she wouldn't return my calls when I wanted her to manage me! I guess one Ozzy is enough for anyone. I still hate what The Osbournes has done to Ozzy's fearsome reputation. We need rock gods more than television shows.
Ginger, the Wildhearts, 2003

Now all you need to make a record is a laptop, one decent microphone and a cool haircut.
Alex James of Blur on Damon Albarn's ability to make a record, 2003

If there is someone I don't want to deal with, I just say, Fuck off. Die. I want you out of my life.

Sharon Osbourne, 2003

> *There's no need to 'countrify' anything or 'popify' anything or 'rockify' anything.*
>
> **Shania Twain, 2003**

Pop Idol TV? I haven't seen anyone on there to really convince me yet. Those kids can sing but you need a bit more to be a pop star than just a good voice. I don't think the shows are an obstacle to real talent getting through. Real talent will get through whatever the obstacles. Look at David Gray. His album beat Gareth Gates to the number one spot didn't it? There's hope yet.

Kim Wilde, 2003

....

I think pop-wise there certainly aren't as many personalities about nowadays as there were in the eighties. That's Robbie Williams' great strength, his personality. It's certainly not his singing! People want performers, personality and drama and you got that in the eighties.

▲ Kim Wilde, 2003

....

Personally, I'd want to see Audioslave rather than Limp Bizkit any day of the week. I don't thing people are going to get any less for their money by not see Fred Durst with his baseball cap on the wrong way.

Bruce Dickinson, Iron Maiden, 2003

....

I don't want to go into what I feel about Roger. I haven't seen him for so long that I don't know what he's like these days. I don't really have any feelings about him.

David Gilmour on ex-Pink Floyd colleague Roger Waters, 2003

....

He doesn't have very many ideas. He's a great guitar player but he's not really a writer.
However conscientious or hard-working Dave was, he would never actually write anything.

Roger Waters, on Dave Gilmour 2003 ▲

....

The thing is with Bruce [Welch], you see, he can't hear me anyway. He used to... even when we had monitors he didn't want to hear me in his monitor, he just wanted to hear himself and the drums. I remember Mark Knopfler guested with us at the Dominion once, went to that side of the stage and said, 'Bruce, you can't hear Hank.' And Bruce said 'nah, I've been working with him for thirty odd-years, I don't wanna hear him.' And Mark said, 'You don't know what you're missing, it sounds great over here!'

Hank Marvin, The Shadows, 2003

....

I miss [Johann]Sebastian Bach like I miss genital warts.

Dave 'Snake' Sabo, Skid Row, 2003

Lars played Fred Durst four songs off our new album and the next week Fred postponed the release of the new Limp Bizkit album and started rewriting it. Lars and I were talking about it: 'Did he postpone it because he wasn't satisfied with it, or did he postpone it because he heard our direction and wanted to be contemporary with it?' It's interesting. We'll see.

Kirk Hammett, Metallica, 2003 ▲

....

Some of that shit sounds like beginners' shit. I understand that they're going for a new, raw and heavy sound, but that's just shit... Lars Ulrich's snare drum is the most irritating thing I've heard in my entire life.

Jonathan Davis, Korn, on Metallica's 'St Anger' album, 2003

....

What the fuck's all that about? We had five albums that were Top Ten! Top Ten singles... Fucking dumbshits over there. Do your homework!

Bobby Blotzer, Dokken, reacts to VH1 preparing 'One Hit Wonders!', 2003

....

Grunge was bad enough, rap metal is really scraping the bottom of the barrel. But even if there was a lot of good music out there I wouldn't listen to it.

Yngwie Malmsteen, 2003

American television has gone absolutely crazy about being gay – girls are kissing girls and boys are kissing boys… They'll be showing breasts next!

David Bowie, 2003

Wanna hear my speech? The BNP are cunts.

Pete Doherty against racism, 2004

This man I will never forgive. It's a small industry and he should hope that he never crosses paths with me because I will rip his head off.
Robin Gibb, Bee Gees, on Graham Norton's joke about the death of Maurice, 2003

You sit and talk about your hopes and your band's music and they say, 'Yeah, that's great. We're really gonna cover your band.' Then you read *The Mirror* and it's like, '1000 pound a day on crack and heroin.' So the five minutes you spent talking about drugs is the article.
Pete Doherty, and the press, 2004 ▲

I don't know if I will ever get over that the Sex Pistols was such a big thing. Every time there's a poll in the papers were the first second or third when it comes to most influential band of all time. You think well great, where's the money? If you beat The Beatles in the league… you think if you got one hundredth of what you got you be doing a lot better than you're doing now.
Glen Matlock, Sex Pistols, 2004

I do wish I ruled the world – I think it'd be a better place.
Courtney Love, 2004

It used to bother me being portrayed as this bitchy person, but now I feel that the public understands me better than some writer. There are people who know who I really am, and that's good enough for me.

Jennifer Lopez, 2004 ▲

The press have written some nasty and spiteful things about the way I look which used to affect me quite badly when it was new to me but luckily, I've learned to ignore the comments. Why do they even care about how I look?

Ex-Spice Girl Melanie Chisholm, 2004

Some of the record companies that were sniffing around would say stuff like, 'How can I be sure that you're not being ironic? How can I market you?' It's just paranoia and ignorance. If you don't like the music, fuck off. Go and drive a bus. This is the entertainment trade, and you need to be entertaining people. If you're not doing that...fuck off and work in a library, you twat.

Justin Hawkins, The Darkness, 2004

We are very tired of each other and it's not fun playing lesbians any more.

Lena Katina, Tatu, 2004

It's pathetic when people swear for the sake of it.
Glen Matlock, ex-Sex Pistol, 2004

Madonna is an old lady. She should get a nice band, just stand in front of them and sing.

Amy Winehouse, 2004

I try to listen to the music channels but you hear stuff where people sing terribly out of tune and they play the wrong notes and chords.
Bill Wyman, 2004

A lot of the time, the British press make me ashamed and embarrassed to be British. They give others the impression that the British are selfish, envious and bitter people, which is simply not true in my opinion. I think that British people in general are really nice and friendly.
Ex-Spice Girl Mel Chisholm, 2004 ▲

The Darkness were really, really inoffensive. I don't know why people hate them or like them. It doesn't do anything for me. I'm not sure if the people who like them do genuinely like them.
Noel Gallagher, 2004

Noel Gallagher is an overrated guitarist losing grip on his credibility who just has to fire desperate shots on his way down. It's kind of a shame, really.
Justin Hawkins, The Darkness 2004

I have a very strong 'no groupies' rule. There's a full-

And when you look at the future of rock'n'roll being in the hands of a band called the fucking Darkness... You know what I mean? This is not an industry I want to be part of.
Fish, ex-Marillion, 2004

If Michael Stipe or Mick Hucknall walked into Pop Idol, they wouldn't get through. They're too ugly.

Louis Walsh, pop manager, 2004

time member of my team whose job it is to make sure I never sleep with a groupie.
Daniel Bedingfield, 2004

single... awesome tour dates... Ozzy strangling Sharon...
Lita Ford, Runaways, 2004

If you pick up a guitar, you don't want to pick it up to learn how to play Oasis songs, you want to learn how to play proper guitar solos.
Justin Hawkins, The Darkness, 2004

I colour my hair but it's certainly nothing Heather suggested. If I want to dye my hair pink, that's up to me and no one else.
▲ Paul McCartney, 2004

Your house is a reflection of yourself, so I want mine to be exquisite.
Britney Spears, 2004

He doesn't pay my rates, and if it was me that was doing this I would have been prosecuted.
Isle of Dogs resident resenting Sir Paul McCartney's noisy rehearsals in the Millennium Dome, 2004

I have many fond memories of Ozzy and Sharon. A top 10

It's all very well Eminem going on about Detroit. You have to be a bit braver to go around singing the praises of Lowestoft.

Justin Hawkins, The Darkness, 2004

> *You know, obviously, I have this sort of strange animal magnetism. It's very hard for me to take my eyes off myself.*

Mick Jagger, 2004

Oasis must have strutted in, four and a half foot tall or whatever they are, thinking, 'Oh God, this country's ours for the taking!' and as soon as it doesn't go their way they go, 'Shall we go back to the UK where we're really popular and successful?' To me it's laziness and arrogance.

Justin Hawkins, The Darkness, 2004

She looks like a cross between someone in a gay club at six in the morning and someone's who's trying to save trees.

Robbie Williams on Christina Aguilera, 2004

She's got a face like a satellite dish!

Robbie Williams on Sophie Ellis Bextor, 2004

I left the Stranglers when the record business was going through a big slump... this looks like the first time in 14 years having a record out properly which is ridiculous. It may sound like I've been sitting around picking my nose and scratching my bum, but in fact I haven't.

▲ Hugh Cornwell, ex-Stranglers, 2004

I expect it'll be like when we turned up in Nottingham the

other day and some bloke said, 'Oh it's that cunt out of the Darkness'. If I'd gone to Lowestoft this time last year it would've been, 'Oh, there's that cunt from school! Get a haircut, soap-dodger!'

Justin Hawkins, The Darkness, 2004

I've been quoted as saying I'd rather stab myself with a plastic fork than sing 'Sex Action'. I'm sure I'm not the only singer who's less than enthusiastic about performing a song they're associated with.

Phil Lewis, LA Guns, 2004 ◄

I don't like the Sun saying 'He's got bad teeth'. But I think 'Yeah, so?' They're white but they're really fucked-up and sharp and that's fine – that's the way I like them. But at the same time it's not a musical criticism, so... now I don't give a shit what anyone says.

Justin Hawkins, The Darkness, 2004

People making *Spinal Tap* comparisons don't know what we're about. We're not some made-up band. We write our own songs. We perform our own songs.

Justin Hawkins, The Darkness 2004

Big Brother is not reality anymore.
You don't get 10 normal people to do it.
You get 10 crap actors in the house.

Simon Cowell, 2004

> *I'll break his fucking nose. I want to know where Simon buys his boots, so I can fill them full of shit and throw them at him.*

Ozzy on Simon Cowell, 2004

Generally you have to ignore anything *NME* writes about us. Recently I met the editor of *NME* and he said to me, 'You are going to hate me when I tell you who I am.' so I said 'Who are you?' and he replied 'I'm the editor of *NME*' to which I said 'Well fuck off then!' because they slagged us off in the early days and we don't do features with them, we don't do anything with them. So they like to have a little dig here and there, but *Kerrang!* have looked after us since the beginning so we are nice to them. *Kerrang!* have got it right, but *NME* are not going to be accurate.

Justin Hawkins, The Darkness 2004

I'm scared for the world. This guy [Bush] is obviously an idiot. He can't speak... I'd do a better job than him – and I'm not very bright!

Robbie Williams, 2004

NME criticised us when we weren't successful. Now we're the biggest band in England and these shits are making fools of themselves by trying to kiss our behinds.

▲ Dan Hawkins, The Darkness 2004

I can't bear political correctness.
I don't like a rule-driven life and I hate the
fact that you can't criticise a fat person.

Simon Cowell, 2004

[My house] is full of Nazi memorabilia.
People say 'I can't go in, I'm half-Jewish.'
I say, my black girlfriend doesn't have a problem,
why should you?

Lemmy, Motörhead, 2004

At least the Latin thing has hit its peak; the Jennifer Lopez and Enrique Iglesias people. They have good songs and they do whatever they do, but it's so Miami, so fucking... gay.'

Rikki Rockett, Poison, 2004 ▲

If you want your body to be healthier, get off the salmonella, e-coli, mad-cow, assembly-line toxic hell train! God I live that statement. What did I just say?

Ted Nugent, 2004

Madonna, best fucking live act? Fuck off! Since when has lip synching been live? Anyone who lip synchs in public on stage when you've paid £75 to see them should be shot. That's me off her Christmas card list, but do I give a toss? NO!

Elton John, 2004

Joe Perry [Aerosmith] used to be one of my favourite guitar players... But then I listen to the crap that they play and I go 'Man, these couldn't be the fucking guys that wrote 'Last Child', 'Back In The Saddle', 'Nodbody's Fault' and 'Sick As A Dog'. Come on!

Dave Mustaine, 2004

'Will there ever be a *Soundgarden Behind The Music?*' No, thank god! I sure as fuck hope not. I really like watching that show but I don't want our band to be a part of that at all, ever.

Matt Cameron, former Soundgarden drummer, 2004 ▲

···

Compare Vince Neil and myself. I went out and wasted money, but I never lost respect for people. Unlike Vince, I never became a boozer, a druggie and never fucked over people. As the story goes, the Ferrari got repossessed and today we're all equal.

Mike Tramp, ex-White Lion, 2004

···

I listened to [*Momentary Lapse Of Reason* and *The Division Bell*] once on each occasion… There wasn't much there, maybe the odd moment when I heard something and thought, 'Well, maybe I'd have done something with that'. I was slightly angry that they managed to get away with it.

When the second one came out… well, it had got totally *Spinal Tap* by then. Lyrics written by the new wife. Well, they are! I mean give me a fucking break! Come on. And what a nerve to call that Pink Floyd. It was an awful record.

Roger Waters, 2004

···

She's a B-movie queen now. She's in all those soft-porn movies. I've distanced myself from that.

Jonathan Cain, Journey, on ex-wife and singer Tane, 2004

*My pants are not as tight any more,
I don't open my shirt so far and I don't
pick up underwear.*

Tom Jones, 2004

My interest in music dissipated during the Eighties as I realised that I was more important.

David Bowie, 2004

There was a time when I ran away from being Wreckless Eric. One of the reasons was I thought everyone hated me, [that was] what I used to get from Stiff Records... it was a way of getting control, I think a lot of people ended up hating the label and it was an extension of that, they hated me as well. I didn't realise that people actually had a lot of respect for me.

Wreckless Eric, 2004

I don't mean to be big-headed, but I don't think we've put a foot wrong in 20 years.

Mike Rutherford, Genesis, 2004

Let the Boy Georges and the George Michaels get up in a twist about it if they don't have the intelligence to see his intelligence.

Sir Elton John on Eminem, 2004

Nikki [Sixx]'s kind of single-handedly fucked up Mötley Crüe, and that's sad.

Vince Neil, ex-Mötley Crüe, 2004

I had bugger all to do with glam rock. When Mott The Hoople started we had long hair and jeans. Being called 'glam' really pisses me off. It devalues the music we are making.

▲ Ian Hunter, 2004

131

We have a website, everyone has a fucking website. Even my grandmother has one – www.nofuckingteeth.com!

Jay Jay French, Twisted Sister, 2004

There are plenty of people earning a living as musicians who weren't born with a gift and have learned how to play, but there are a lot of mediocre musicians out there, no doubt about it.

Robin Trower, 2004

....

When I cut my hair, I end up looking like a waitress from Santa Monica. There's something wrong with curly hair when it's cut short.

Robin Plant,
Led Zeppelin, 2004 ▶

....

How could you Eric? We used to call you God. We thought you were a hard-edged rocker committed to the blues, with the occasional acid trip thrown in. What went wrong? I loved you, Eric, but to go from 'Spoonful' and 'Crossroads' to 'Wonderful Tonight' in just one lifetime is too much.

Bernie Tormé on Eric Clapton,
2004

....

Paul Stanley decided to make fun out of me when I was a little kid, in the middle of a crowd of Kiss fans, so I always thought he was a cunt for that.

Ginger, the Wildhearts, 2004

....

Scott [Weiland] always wants to work, and that's a change. With Axl it was impossible to get him to do anything. Scott's whole problem is tangible – it's just a drug problem, it's not something completely insane that we can't understand.

Slash, velvet revolver/ex-Guns N'Roses, 2004 ◥

Downloading worries me a lot. In my opinion it's theft. The record companies should have got involved a long time ago and produced a system to help police downloading. Musicians get gas bills, too, and they have to eat; not all of them are loaded.

Tommy Vance, DJ, 2004

We say we made a deal with the Devil. See, I love that, and I think it's hilarious. We're serious musicians, but we can still be Spinal Tap. You have to be, otherwise you lose your mind like other people in rock'n'roll.

Rob Halford, Judas Priest, 2004

I'm no expert on film, I'm no columnist, I'm a guy who likes a good movie and I'm sick and tired of walking out of a theatre, being CGI'd to death.

Henry Rollins 2004

We refer to gay people as faggots…
Women who like women, that's cool.

50 Cent, 2004

The Kurt Cobains and Keith Richards of this world are so appealing to a critic. They think they're the real thing. You live vicariously through them until they kill themselves. So if someone is bald and wears a wig, they can't be the real thing. Or you can't play great rock if you're rich. These are creeds started by frustrated journalists!

Paul Stanley, Kiss, 2004 ▲

....

Nobody can tell me I suck, because I simply don't believe it.

Perry Farrell, Jane's Addiction, 2004

....

I heard she's got really ugly toes – that her feet are crazy-looking. I'm a foot man, so when I heard that I was like, I don't know if I'm gonna see it [DVD]. I heard her feet are up in the camera, a lot of these crazy feet shots.

Tommy Lee, Mötley Crüe, on Paris Hilton's feet, 2004

....

We made a decision a long time ago to not be like Led Zeppelin or Kiss, not to be a band with a mystique around it. That comes from our punk roots.

Lars Ulrich, Metallica, 2004

....

When travelling in England avoid the Little Chefs. Even if they are the only thing open.

Danny Vaughn, Tyketto, 2004

*When I see some of these hip hop videos
I'm as horrified as my grandmother and
think, 'Oh God, what are they doing there?'*

Kylie Minogue, 2004

Wearing jeans and T-shirts is a symbol of white American imperialism, like drinking Coca-Cola.

Björk, 2004

Lenny [Wolf] was impossible to deal with. He was German and he had a very limited vocabulary and he thought he was God.

Producer Keith Olsen recalling Kingdom Comes's *Kingdom Come* album, 2004

....

When the world is going nuts you want a guy who is nuttier than them.

Gene Simmons on George Bush, 2004

....

I'm just sick and tired of Christmas hysteria. I don't want presents because there is nothing I need and I don't want to give any because of all the hassle.

Jim Lea, Slade, 2004

....

Seriously, at first I was happy for them, but now I find it a little irritating. I think they trivialise what we do, and punk rock in general. It's like throwing shit in the face of something or someone that had substance at one point. Didn't one of the members marry someone from MTV? I mean, what the fuck? But if any band should be pissed off at them then isn't NOFX.

Mike Dirnt, Green Day, on Blink-182, 2004

....

Never say never. If we're all skint with seven kids when we're 25, then maybe.

▲ Matt Willis, Busted, on a reunion, 2004

....

I'm rebelling against myself. I've taken out all my piercings apart from one in my right nipple. That's for me.

Christina Aguilera, 2004

....

It's really sad. He's so young I don't think that he's going to listen to anybody. I don't think the people around him set a good example, which is a shame. I have to be very discreet what I say, but I just think he was really nervous on the day. But, you know, he had his chance to do it and he came on... at least he looked great!

Elton John, on Pete Doherty's appearance at Live8, 2005

....

I don't buy that idea that you need to have had a hard life to make that kind of music. OK, I'm rich and famous, I've got a lovely family and a lovely boyfriend. Although I have had hard times, I'm just not a tortured soul. Mind you, Pete Doherty's not that good anyway. Creates all this misery for himself to write songs and then doesn't even turn up to play them.

Charlotte Church, 2005

....

He [Doherty] is a genius. But I've known many people like that and they're all dead.

◀ Roger Daltrey, 2005

....

I wouldn't even think about playing music if I was born in these times. I'd probably turn to something like mathematics.

Bob Dylan, 2004

Bob Geldof has organised this amazing global event, I was facing 210,000 people, the cameras are rolling, and fucking Elton John is duetting with me. And Bob's daughter has secretly made a pass at me. It's all I can think about. It did my head in. I didn't think Bob would be very happy.

Pete Doherty, on Live8, 2005 ▲

Pete [Doherty] – calm down a little and start checking yourself. You're not impressing anyone. You're depressing.

John Lydon, 2005

What can you say about Pete Doherty? If you have to take heroin to be famous – well, I don't get it. Will Pete be a Kurt Cobain or a Jimi Hendrix? Never in a million years. He hasn't the talent to tune their guitars.

Pete Waterman, 2005

I'd say firstly [Pete Doherty] doesn't do rock music, and secondly, he only sells records because people are curious as to what a junkie sounds like. I think that's really wrong and really irresponsible... I think he's a talentless waste of fucking skin!

Justin Hawkins, The Darkness, 2005

Pete Doherty? Well he needs a bleedin' good slap, that's

I don't know what Kate Moss sees in him.

Justin Hawkins on Pete Docherty, 2005

He thinks no-one understands him but of course we all do. You're just being a wanker. Go home.

Charlotte Church on Pete Docherty, 2005

what. He needs locking down in rehab for a couple of months.

Sharon Osbourne, 2005

....

I don't really like punk. Most of it is crap. What I like is considered quite cheesy – Boston, Queen, Slade. In my punk days, I could never have admitted to liking bands like that. I'd have been given a beating.

Steve Jones, Sex Pistols, 2005 ▲

I despise hip hop. 50 Cent is the most distasteful character I've met.

Noel Gallagher, 2005

....

Fucking Babyshambles. I don't want to fight them, I don't want their fucking birds, I don't want to shoot their dogs, don't want to stand on their hamster's head and I'm just not into their music.

Liam Gallagher, 2005

....

I didn't understand why everybody who was trying to coax me in happened to be knighted. I got hit on by Sir Bob [Geldof] and Sir Mick [Jagger], but I said to Mick 'We ain't doing it pal. You can do it, but I ain't.'

Keith Richards on Live8, 2005

....

When I was that age, there was no such thing as binge drinking.

Shirley Bassey, on fellow Cardiff girl
Charlotte Church, 2005

*I didn't fancy Britney (Spears) that much.
She walks like Charlie Chaplin.*

Chat-show host Frank Skinner, 2005

I would love for the time to come where somebody can talk about me and not have to talk about Britney and Christina in the same sentence. We're really, really different.

Jessica Simpson, 2005

By the time we made 'Brave New World' I was desperate to leave the huge popularity I was receiving. In 1980 we did three university tours and they were raw and energetic and I loved that, by 1982 I'd become a merchandise name and I really wasn't enjoying that at all.

Toyah Wilcox, 2005 ▲

I mentioned to Bob [Geldof] I could make love for eight hours. What I didn't say was that this included four hours of begging and then dinner and a movie.

Sting, 2005

There are a lot of shit bands out there. The White Stripes – I just don't get that.

Nicky Wire, Manic Street Preachers, 2005

I'm bored with music between 1955 and 1980. I'm completely bored. I can't listen to a rock and roll record. I can't do it. I would rather listen to hogs screwing.

Sting, 2005

People forget you very quickly.
Look at Kim Wilde. She became a gardener.

Will Young on celebrity shelf life, 2005

I'd rather vote for a chimpanzee than Bush.

Sting, 2005

What do you get when you put two brothers and two sisters in a band? A big fat melting pot of talent.

Top Of The Pops host Richard Bacon on The Magic Numbers, 2005

....

They won't last unless they develop a sense of humour. Or a diet that works.

MP Ann Widdecome on The Magic Numbers, 2005

....

Commercials are an unnatural use of my work… it's like having a cow's udder sewn to the side of my face. Painful and humiliating.

Tom Waits, 2005 ▶

....

It's funny, because when

you're on tour, from the beginning of the day to the end of the day you're just working. And so during the day, sometimes you're stressed or pissed off and you might snap at somebody. You asked for something and it doesn't arrive within, like, five minutes… [Laughs] You end up following people around apologizing a lot. 'I'm really sorry. I'm so sorry.' But I guess it's just stress, isn't it?

Guy Berryman, Coldplay, 2005

....

I'm not sure why she's so successful. Maybe it's the fact that she was always naked.

Brian Wilson on Madonna, 2005

....

Pete Doherty is the ultimate rock'n'roll fuckwit.

Pete Townshend, The Who, 2006

I don't hold any grudges and have nothing against the people of Leeds, but we did really well last year and a pat on the back would have been nice.

Kaiser Chief Ricky Wilson on losing Rock Band of the Year at Leeds Music Awards, 2005

To shred without any substance is interesting for a second, it's fascinating. But if the music doesn't have any substance to it... I don't regret popularising anything – it's like telling Nirvana do you regret popularising grunge? Look what you've done, you've created an ocean of horrific shit, bands that are just trying to pantomime your genius! At least, that's what I heard all through the nineties after Nirvana came on the scene.

Steve Vai, 2005

It's not impossible another singer could come along that I might want to do a project with, but it's unlikely. I don't want to have my vision diluted by anything. When I pull other people into the mix, for better or worse it changes. I don't want it to change, I want it to be my vision.

▲ Steve Vai, 2005

The Stones said that every time they put out an album they think it's their best and they can't understand why people don't take the new records as seriously as the old ones. Well, you're old age pensioners. By all means make records and go on tour, because if people want to see you, fine, but don't expect to be taken seriously. Your best work is behind you.

Noel Gallagher, Oasis, 2006

....

I've played with some legends that that I have some great memories with, and met some legends that I wish I hadn't met. One of them, who's a major, major superstar came to see us play in Wales a couple of years ago, and we were all very nervous that he was in the crowd. We were in the middle of the show and my roadie comes up to me and says 'You'll never guess who's here to hear you tonight'. Afterwards we went into the dressing room and met him, and he was drunk to the point of... all he did was go 'arghhh' at us, and pass out on the couch in our dressing room.

▲ Walter Trout, 2005

....

That'll be a good night. It's funny, you rarely hear actors slagging each other off but with musicians it's almost the done thing.

Will Young on the Baftas, 2005

Most priests are gay.

Madonna, 2006

I was sitting next to him and he pointed to the cameraman and was like, 'Hey you, why don't you point that camera at me and put it on the screen so I can see how good I look?' I've never heard a guy say that. That was the first thing I heard him say. I thought, 'Who is that dude?'

Pink on Charlotte Church's other half, rugby star Gavin Henson, 2006 ▲

....

Craig David's gone a bit middle of the road. It's a bit Elton John. Arctic Monkeys? Wouldn't know if I fell over them. Dizzee Rascal is a bit

much for me. He sounds like 12-year-old boy on the brink of puberty.

Charlotte Church, 2006

....

Making movies is such an effort, and to do that over and over again, with the possibility that I am going to get the shit kicked out of me – and they really enjoy doing it – I mean, it doesn't make sense. I have sort of let it go.

Madonna, 2006

....

Many people become so boring when they get kids, they seem to want to take over the house you live in.

I thought, I wish this writer extreme misery and bodily harm.

Gwyeth Paltrow on journalists criticising her husband Chris Martin's band Coldplay, 2006

You have to be quiet when the babies are asleep... fuck that! It's my house and I am the boss in my house.

Noel Gallagher on children, 2006

....

I think it's ridiculous, actually. Mick and Keith should get a life. It's like a strange, sexual compulsion. How much do they need? I think a lot of it is the applause. It's a powerful drug, 50,000 people appearing to adore you'.

David Gilmour, ex-Pink Floyd, 2006 ▲

....

There's this whole thing going on at the moment with Blair and the nuclear thing.

This all started kicking off about two or three weeks before I was supposed to meet with Blair, which I was not happy about anyway for obvious reasons, ie Iraq. It was, 'If we could just have a meeting beforehand where we could go through how it would proceed...' It was like talking to Blair's spin doctors. It was all getting weird. It was just obvious there was no point in meeting him anyway, and I didn't want to. Luckily, in the end the decision was kind of made for me.

Thom Yorke on refusing to meet Tony Blair to discuss global warning, 2006

....

I like Gorillaz. I mean obviously Damon's a cunt – but don't write that – but they're great.

Alex James, Blur 2006

Why would I want to meet this man?

Thom Yorke, Radiohead, turning down Tony Blair's invitation to Downing Street, 2006

I'm from Tennessee.
Some of us don't have teeth, let alone an iPod.

Justin Timberlake, 2006

I can't see the [Rolling Stones] going on too much longer, I really can't. It's getting a bit ridiculous, innit? It's their lives. But I don't know if they've got anything else that's important to 'em outside that apart from families. Mick will never answer a question properly. He doesn't like to talk about the past. He can't stay in one place for more than a couple of weeks, and then he has to be off somewhere else. I don't think he's happy.

Bill Wyman, 2006

The Rolling Stones are old men trying to be young guys.
Fabrizio Moretti, the Strokes, 2006

Libertines gigs were full of private-school kids. Their music was pretentious.
◀ Alex Turner, Arctic Monkeys, 2006

Kim will take everything. She'll go through all his money. She wouldn't want to get married so quick if he'd got a pre-nup. Kim is very controlling. She's turned him against his family.
Eminem's grandmother Betty Kresin, 2006

I have wisdom, I feel love, I love in the present and I try to present a dimension that brings harmony and healing. My concept is the opposite of George W Bush. There is more value in placing a flower in a rifle barrel than making war. As Jimi Hendrix used to say, musical notes have more importance than bullets.

Carlos Santana, 2006 ▲

If you guys think I'm a diva, Snoop is like next-level hip-hop king. His requirements... are like, beyond platinum edition.

Mariah Carey, 2006

It has been 18 years since [The Smiths] ended; I don't know them, they don't know me, they know nothing about me, I know nothing about them. Anything I know about them is unpleasant, so why on earth do we want to be on stage together making music? I would rather eat my own testicles than reform The Smiths, and that's saying something for a vegetarian.

Morrissey, 2006

If Prince was from Wigan, he would have been slaughtered by now.

Morrissey, 2006

I've been working so hard, I'm about to have a Mariah Carey.

Usher, 2006

Long hair is an unpardonable offence which should be punishable by death.

Morrissey, 2006

*If I met Vic Reeves, I'd have no desire
other than to smack him in the face.*

Morrissey, 2006

It's happening all too quickly for [the Arctic Monkeys]. They haven't proved a thing and they haven't had to work very hard – that must make them insecure. It's all a bit unnatural. OK they've sold about 700,000 albums, but it can't be gratifying. They haven't been driving up and down the M1 for fifteen years.

Morrissey, 2006

....

I'm sorry that the comments I made at SouthBy SouthWest about the Arctic Monkeys were printed so harshly in the *Times* and the *NME*. I actually quite like the Arctic Monkeys and whatever I said

was said with tender, avuncular concern. I hope to God I didn't upset their grannies. In any case, I was wrong about their success being too sudden and without any dues paid, because that's exactly how it happened for The Smiths. So, I really should shut it.

Morrissey, 2006

....

It's more the quality argument – you can get 15,000 tracks on your iPod, and people just want to fill it. They're not bothered about what the songs are. Nobody takes music to heart – it's all about having it.

▲ Jarvis Cocker, 2006

....

*Younger men make you listen to Coldplay –
and there ain't no treatment for that.*

Jerry Hall, 2006

I can't listen to that stuff. They don't have a good sound... Jack's half into the sound and music, but then he wants to be a pop star as well, so you've got a big problem.

Billy Childish on The White Stripes, 2006

....

Billy Childish; Meg and I really feel sorry for you. It must be lonely sitting in all of that garage rock bitterness Billy. You know children, when you take someone else's music and put your own lyrics on top of it, it's still called plagiarism. Something Mister Childish hasn't learned yet.... By the way Billy, we didn't have to have you play with us, and we didn't have to mention you in interviews, we were just being polite in a foreign land. But you're welcome anyways. The bitter garage rocker...

▲ **Jack White, White Stripes, 2006**

....

Though I have undoubtedly angered Jack White, I think it's a bit nasty of him to accuse me of plagiarism merely because his former admiration of my work was not reciprocated. It all smacks of jealousy to me. I have a bigger collection of hats, a better moustache, a more blistering guitar sound and a fully developed sense of humour. The only thing I can't understand is why I'm not rich. Yours sincerely, Billy Childish.

P.S. I always stay well within the music industries recommended guidelines of never plagiarising more than 50% of my material. But no matter who my influences may be, I would never stoop so low as to rip off Led Zeppelin. P.P.S I hope I've gone and offended Led Zeppelin now.

▼ Billy Childish, 2006

Oooof. Just seen a review of ours from *FHM* magazine regarding our new album... Apparently we make Radiohead sound like the Cheeky Girls. Boom Boom! Surely that's a compliment coming from a New Man who probably wears a handbag and has every Cheeky Girls song on his pink iPod Nano.

Barry Burns, Mogwai, 2006

He did send me a letter apologising for his last outburst, right before his wedding. But he seems to be angry. I seem to have become a target. It's not very gentlemanly or gracious.

Madonna on Elton John's outburst, 2006

Canada has placed itself alongside China as the cruellest and most self-serving nation. We will not include any Canadian dates on our world tour to promote our new album. This is in protest against the barbaric slaughter of over 325,000 baby seals which is now underway. I fully realise that the absence of any Morrissey concerts in Canada is unlikely to bring the Canadian economy to its knees, but it is our small protest against this horrific slaughter – which is the largest slaughter of marine animal species found anywhere on the planet.
Morrissey, 2006

....

Gwen [Stefani] sort of has a perkiness and a smartness that's pleasant. We've always said the worst thing about her is that she's married to the guy [Gavin Rossdale] from Bush. I'm sure he's a nice guy, but his band is so repulsive.

▲ Wayne Coyne, Flaming Lips, 2006

....

A good thing for new music would be more of the mainstream loosening up a bit and letting stuff through. Radio 1 won't play anything

They look like the Railway Children.
Kasabian man Serge Pizzorno on Franz Ferdinand, 2006

*They [USA tour promoters] asked for my passport
to prove I was a woman.*
Annie Lennox, 2006

You fat, Boxtox-faced, wig-wearin' fuck!

Velvet Revolver singer Scott Weiland on Axl Rose, 2006

fucking decent. You need to sort the radio out. The fact that poor Arctic Monkeys are getting so much attention is purely based on the fact that the mainstream music business is such a bunch of fucking retards as far as I'm concerned.

Thom Yorke, 2006

It's like people who say they don't like McDonald's. You just think 'Who the fuck are you? You're crazy!' McDonald's is bad for you, but it's wonderful. It's like smoking crack or something.

Wayne Coyne, The Flaming Lips, 2006

It's a travesty. We're going to get some middle of the road weepy ballad. That's definitely not going to get anyone singing along on the terraces, is it? Embrace just don't do it for me. They should have got Arctic Monkeys with Wayne Rooney rapping along, otherwise the FA should have just re-issued 'World In Motion'.

▲ Peter Hook, New Order, on Embrace's England World Cup song, 2006

I like about three records of his. The rest of it's pish.

Paul Weller on David Bowie, 2006

*He said he wanted to bring ballet
to the working classes. What a cunt.*

Paul Weller on Freddie Mercury, 2006

It can't be for his music, man. I mean, if it's for his charity work in Africa then you can't knock it, but Boomtown Rats, fuck off.

Paul Weller, 2006, on Bob Geldof winning the Outstanding Achievement Award

....

The whole thing of Bono becoming the Pope – what the fuck's all that about?

Pseudo-American rubbish.
Paul Weller on Bono, 2006

....

Fucking horrible man. Not my cup of tea at all. Fucking rubbish. No edge, no attitude, no nothing.

Paul Weller on Sting, 2006

....

I was on stage in Dublin when I heard a girl in the crowd shout: 'KT, you're a lesbian!' What the hell do you say to that? I didn't want to upset the lesbians but I didn't want to make out I was one. I said: 'You can't say that!' Then I realised that none of the other 1,500 people there had heard her. So I said: 'That girl just called me a lesbian'. At the end of the gig, a roadie handed me a note from the woman. It said: 'KT, I was saying legend.'

▲ KT Tunstall, 2006

....

I was never asked to do a duet with Paul Weller so I've no idea why he made those comments. I don't care.

James Blunt, 2006

> *He shouldn't be behind a wheel at all –*
> *he should employ a chauffeur.*

MP Robert Goodwill on George Michael's driving exploits

Might I suggest that those selling their tickets on eBay for stupid money give a contribution... say 30 percent of their proceeds back to Friends Of The Earth, for whose benefit we are all doing this show? Seems only fair, unless you're a shallow... don't you think?'

Thom Yorke, 2006, on internet touts selling Radiohead charity concert tickets

Sometimes I wish I wasn't so much at home alone and that it wasn't about nannies and chauffeurs and all that stuff.

I get to meet everyone I want and I get quite a lot of attention because of it, you know? But of course it hurts when you see a lot of lies about her in tabloids and then you think, 'Well, it's not that cool to have a cool mom.' I don't like seeing my mom upset. No one does, right?

Frances Bean Cobain [13], 2006

Us and McFly are going to kick his arse. [Harry Potter actor] Daniel Radcliffe talks a lot of shit. He keeps talking about everyone else's talent but he should look at his own – he is atrocious.

▲ James Bourne, Son of Dork, 2006

I'm English and I'm gay, so obviously I'm mad. And all celebrities have periods where they lose their marbles.

Boy George, 2006

He [Radcliffe]'s slagged us off in interviews – we've never met him, so I don't know where it's coming from. He's going to be embarrassed when he does meet us.

Dougie Poynter, McFly, 2006 ▲

It's happened to us when we've slagged off people we haven't met and when we do meet them we just feel stupid – that's how we want him to feel. [Radcliffe] said about us: 'I know bands who can actually play their instruments and who write their songs.' Well, we know actors who play more than one character. He's got his facts wrong.

Tom Fletcher, McFly, 2006

I hate them. If I wasn't forced to go, I wouldn't bother attending. It's just a strange event – so many egos in one room. I'm chuffed to be nominated but it's not my kind of thing.

Will Young on the Brits, 2006

If I don't win Album of the Year, I'm gonna have a problem with that... I said I was the face of the Grammys last year. This year I'm 10 times that!

Kanye West, 2006

I don't want my nipples looking for coins on the street.

Sharon Osbourne on plastic surgery, 2006

Does he really know what he does with these kids?
I don't want to tell you my brother's innocent.
I am not certain that he is.

Jermaine Jackson on brother Michael, 2006

Piccadilly Radio played a record of mine and the DJ said 'Ah Tony Christie whatever happened to him? We've not heard from him for a long time,' and someone rang in and said 'He's dead!' That was about ten years ago... it might have been wishful thinking!

Tony Christie, 2006 ◥

....

The band? It's over. Reunited because of the good cause, to get over the bad relationship, and not to have regrets. I think I've had enough. I am 60. I don't want to work much anymore. It's an important part of my life, I have had enormous satisfactions, but now it's enough. It's much more comfortable to work on my own.

The issue about Roger is irrelevant, because even without him I don't want to go on as Pink Floyd. I'm happy with my life. Playing as Pink Floyd is a business too big for me now. When you move as a band, all is gigantic, the expectations are enormous, the pressures very high.

We have been asked to play one hundred gigs! I am fine as I live now. It was fantastic but now I don't feel like it any more.

David Gilmour, 2006

....

I had a horrifying, frightful encounter with the paparazzi while I was with my baby. Because of a recent incident when I was trapped in my car without my baby by a throng of paparazzi, I was terrified that this time the physically aggressive paparazzi would put both me and my baby in danger. I instinctively took measures to get my baby and me out of harm's way,

but the paparazzi continued to stalk us, and took photos of us which were sold to the media. I love my child and would do anything to protect him.

Britney Spears, 2006, after appearing to show her driving with her five-month-old son on her lap

....

I'm not watching Muse after what he said about me mum. It were in New York and me mum goes to him, 'Oh, I like your band.' And what did he say? 'That she were fit!'

▲ Andy Nicholson, Arctic Monkeys, 2006

....

My audience loves to see Britney [Spears] get her head cut off.

Alice Cooper, on his stage show, 2006

> *It's very, very tough to engage in three bored judges as we normally are on American Idol.*
> Simon Cowell, 2006

They are idiots are they not? They're fucking idiots... they're small, noisy, smelly, small, devil brats! They take too much time and they cry all the time.

The new thing, which wasn't in *Pop Idol* four years ago, is the emphasis on 'This show will change your life and you'll be a better person.' A lot of people on these shows are really nice but there's the message that fame and money will make them better people and that's so unhealthy. When I did *Pop Idol* it was about seeing who could sing.
Will Young on *X-Factor*, 2006

They're superficial. He actually sings about things that Arctic Monkeys do but they do it in a way that's very meaningful, whereas Hard-Fi do it in a way that's really bland.

▲ Will, Mystery Jets, 2006

99% of the people who turn up [to *American Idol*] are completely and utterly hopeless – that they get worse every year and this year's the worst of the lot. I would also say Paula [Abdul, fellow judge] is making less sense this year than she's ever done.
Simon Cowell, 2006

There's nothing more funny than seeing someone who's, like, right famous.

Jamie Cook, Arctic Monkeys, 2006

*Basically rock stardom comes down
to the cut of your trousers.*

David Bowie, 2006

[Arctic Monkey] Alex Turner does it in a way that's beautiful, but [Hard Fi] Richard Archer does it in a really laddish, obvious way. Watching the way he performs, he makes me feel uncomfortable and it makes me think 'right, so that's what a man is? That's what a man should be like?' – the way he's leaning into girls' faces shouting 'awwight poppet!' I don't wanna go there... they come from about a mile down the road from us and their fans are probably harder than our fans, but I don't care. We're the anti-Hard-Fi, basically!

Blaine Harrison, Mystery Jets, 2006 ▲

When I was writing these songs, I found myself thinking about a lot of people like Destiny's Child and the Black Eyed Peas, people like Britney Spears and Gwen Stefani, which is sort of strange for me.

There's a line in [one] song that goes, 'So go tell Britney and go tell Gwen,' and I guess part of what I'm railing against on that song is this preternaturally happy music sung by kids and written by 40-year-old Swedish men. And in between them there's this void. I guess the worst offender is like the Black Eyed Peas or Destiny's Child, where they're going, 'I'm a survivor, I'm gonna make it,' and I'm like, 'Well, you're 20, what are you going to survive? Getting a bikini wax this weekend?"

Wayne Coyne, Flaming Lips, 2006

....

I'd rather have a small following of really cool people who get it, who will grow with us as we grow and are fans for life, than people that have us in their five-disc changer with Reba McEntire and Toby Keith. We don't want those kinds of fans. They limit what you can do.

Martie Maguire, Dixie Chicks, 2006 ▲

....

The problem with *American*

Idol, if there is a problem, is that it's like buying a lottery ticket. The chances of winning it are really remote. I would actually say, get some experience. Do the hard gigs. Do a tough audience. And learn how to handle a difficult audience before you walk into an audition room with us sitting there as judges. My second bit of advice would be don't bother. Because you've got to be fantastic nowadays to do well on a show like *Idol*. You know, good isn't good enough. And they're not great odds. You've got to be great.

Simon Cowell, 2006

....

Pop Idol is worse than terrorism.

Morrissey, 2006

Rave is the refuge for the mentally deficient. It's made by dull people for dull people.

Morrissey, 2006

I heard [the Kooks'] single on the radio the other day and it sounds like fucking Avril Lavigne! If he can live with himself after that production, and if he feels like he has to slag people off to keep up, then I'm sure his nights are long and those moments of doubt are really painful. For a start, he models his style on me. And that record is the most horrible thing I've ever heard. It sounds like the band are literally rolling over, sticking their arse in the air and begging Radio 1 to fuck them. So fuck The Kooks. Fuck 'em!

▼ Johnny Borrell, Razorlight, on The Kooks, 2006

I have to ask myself the question when I came over here, does a Brit deserve to judge Americans? Then I thought, actually, a good voice is a good voice. But I've had over 100 Number One records. I've sold over 200 million records. So based on the success of that, I probably am qualified. But it's a subjective business.

Simon Cowell, 2006

Festivals are about rock music.
It's like, to me, Kylie playing Glastonbury
would be the ultimate insult to it.

Lily Allen, 2006

INDEX